THE ITALIAN RENAISSANCE

PAUL ROBERT WALKER

Facts On File®

AN INFOBASE HOLDINGS COMPANY

On the cover: *School of Athens*, Raphael (1509–11). This Renaissance fresco shows the ancient philosophers Plato and Aristotle in the center. Plato points toward heaven, indicating the nature of his speculations, while Aristotle points to the physical world before him.

The Italian Renaissance

Copyright © 1995 by Paul Robert Walker

Facts On File, Inc.
460 Park Avenue South
New York, NY 10016

Library of Congress Cataloging-in-Publication Data

Walker, Paul Robert.
 The Italian Renaissance / Paul Robert Walker.
   p. cm. — (World history library)
 Includes bibliographical references and index.
 ISBN 0-8160-2942-3
   1. Italy—Civilization—1268–1559. 2. Renaissance—Italy.
 I. Title. II. Series.
 DG533.W35 1995
 945—dc20   94–34605

Facts On File books are available at special discounts when purchased in bulk quantities for businesses, associations, institutions or sales promotions. Please call our Special Sales Department in New York at 212/683-2244 or 800/322-8755.

Text design by Donna Sinisgalli
Cover design by Amy Gonzalez
Map by Dale Williams
Printed in the United States of America

MP FOF 10 9 8 7 6 5 4 3 2 1

This book is printed on acid-free paper.

To the spirit of the Italian
Renaissance and those who share
it—past, present, and future.

By Paul Robert Walker

Hoop Dreams
Nonfiction for young adults
(Based on the documentary film)

Who Invented the Game?
with Geoffrey C. Ward and Ken Burns
Photo-illustrated nonfiction (BASEBALL: The American Epic)

Spiritual Leaders
Biographies for young adults (American Indian Lives series)

Big Men, Big Country: A Collection of American Tall Tales
Illustrated fiction for young readers

Head for the Hills! The Amazing True Story of the Johnstown Flood
Nonfiction for young readers (Read It to Believe It! series)

The Sluggers Club: A Sports Mystery
A middle-grade novel

Bigfoot and Other Legendary Creatures
Illustrated fiction/nonfiction for young readers

Great Figures of the Wild West
Biographies for young adults (American Profiles series)

The Method
A young adult novel

Pride of Puerto Rico: The Story of Roberto Clemente
Biography for young readers

CONTENTS

AUTHOR'S NOTE

History has two sides. There is reality: the actual events and achievements that occur during a particular historical period. Then there is the perception of that reality, both by the people who live through the period and by those who look back at it. Until fairly recently, our view of the Italian Renaissance has been shaped by the Swiss historian Jacob Burckhardt, whose brilliant study, *The Civilization of the Renaissance in Italy,* was first published in 1860. Burckhardt saw Renaissance Italy as the "leader of modern ages," a time when the rediscovery of the cultural heritage of Greece and Rome led to a new and more modern way of looking at the world. For Burckhardt, there was a definite line between the Renaissance and the Middle Ages, marked by the development of individualism:

> In the Middle Ages both sides of human consciousness—that which was turned within as that which was turned without—lay dreaming or half awake beneath a common veil. The veil was woven of faith, illusion, and childish prepossession, through which the world and history were seen clad in strange hues. Man was conscious of himself only as a member of a race, people, party, family, or corporation—only through some general category. In Italy this veil melted into air; an *objective* treatment and consideration of the State and of all the things of this world became possible. The *subjective* side at the same time asserted itself with

corresponding emphasis; man became a spiritual *individual* and recognized himself as such.

During the 1960s, historians began to reinvestigate and reinterpret the events of the Renaissance, and today scholars consider the line between the Middle Ages and the Renaissance to be much hazier. There is a new respect for the substantial achievements of the Middle Ages, and a new realization that many developments we once associated with the Renaissance actually began during the earlier period. At the same time, there is a realization that many aspects of the Renaissance period were not modern at all. Some historians take this to such an extreme that they practically deny that the Renaissance ever happened. But this seems an overreaction to Burckhardt's oversimplification. The truth lies somewhere in between.

Certainly the people of the Renaissance believed they were living in a new and exciting age. The 15th-century humanist Matteo Palmieri exulted that he had been "born in this new age, so full of hope and promise, which already rejoices in a greater array of nobly-gifted souls than the world has seen in the thousand years that have preceded it." The sheer volume of brilliance in Renaissance Italy makes it one of the great ages of human achievement, and this undeniable outpouring of individual creativity is far more important than the precise, scholarly definition of historical periods. The fact is this: Something amazing happened in Italy between around 1300 and 1550, and we call it the Italian Renaissance.

Because development occurred at different times in different cities and in different areas of human achievement, it's impossible to present a history of the Italian Renaissance from start to finish in a strictly chronological format. Yet, a period that spans some 250 years needs a clear sense of time, for Italy was a very different place in the year 1550 than it was in 1300. So this book is organized both by chronology and by subject. For each city or subject area, the account is essentially chronological, but there is some overlapping and backtracking as we move from city to city or subject to subject.

Chapter 1 presents the important developments of the late Middle Ages that set the stage for the Renaissance, bringing the story to around the year 1300. Chapter 2 covers key events and cultural achievements during the 14th century, a period that some historians call the "proto-Renaissance" but that I've simply called the "early Renaissance." Chapters 3 through 6 present the blossoming of Renaissance culture in the most important city-states, while Chapters 7 through 10 examine various cultural and intellectual subject areas. Finally, Chapters 11 and 12 return to the larger story with a chronological account of the foreign invasions and the spread of Renaissance culture to northern Europe.

Anyone who writes history ultimately comes face to face with his or her own interests, especially in a book like this, where a huge sweeping period is covered in relatively few words. It's impossible to include every important event, person, or idea, so difficult choices must be made. Although I tried to remain objective, I'll gladly admit to my own intellectual prejudice: like Jacob Burckhardt, I'm fascinated by the development of individuality and individual creative expression. And, though I recognize the truth in more recent Renaissance scholarship, I firmly believe that the Italian Renaissance was a great new age of individual expression.

The people of the Renaissance felt they were discovering themselves in the culture of ancient Greece and Rome. Writing at the tail end of the 20th century, I felt that I was rediscovering *my*self in the culture of the Renaissance. I hope that you do, too.

Paul Robert Walker
Escondido, California
July 1994

Italy During the Renaissance

1 MARQUISATE OF SALUZZO
2 MONTFERRAT
3 INDEPENDENT STATES
4 REPUBLIC OF MANTUA

SAVOY

Milan
Po R.
Verona
Padua
Mantua
Adige R.
Venice

MILAN
Parma
Genoa
Ferrara

MODENA
Bologna

FERRARA

GENOA
Lucca

LUCCA
Florence
Rimini
Pisa
Arno R.
Urbino

FLORENCE
Siena

PAPAL
Assisi

SIENA
STATES

CORSICA

Tiber R.
Rome

Garigliano R.

Naples
KINGDOM
OF
NAPLES

SARDINIA

REPUBLIC OF VENICE

ADRIATIC SEA

TYRRHENIAN SEA

MEDITERRANEAN SEA

N

SCALE
0   40   80   120 Miles

Palermo

SICILY

Italy in 1454, when the Peace of Lodi began a 40-year period of relative stability on the Italian peninsula.

SEEDS OF THE RENAISSANCE:

History, Geography, Wealth, and Freedom

The Italian Renaissance was an age of genius, a time when human beings reached a new level of self-expression. In many ways, the Renaissance was the beginning of the modern world. Even today—almost 500 years after the height of the Renaissance—we look at the paintings of Leonardo and Raphael or the sculpture of Donatello and Michelangelo and see our own reflection.

Although we usually think of the Renaissance as an age of great art, it was also an age of greatness in other areas. Renaissance rulers like Lorenzo de' Medici developed politics and diplomacy to a new level of sophistication, and the brilliant writer Niccolò Machiavelli defined a political philosophy still practiced by presidents and prime ministers today. Bankers and merchants established a modern economic system, physicians laid the foundation for modern medicine, and architects combined art and new technology to create beautiful buildings. Teachers used new methods of education, while men and women followed new rules of social behavior.

Where did all this "newness" come from? There are many answers to this question, but the first answer may be surprising: it came from the past.

Renaissance is a French word meaning "rebirth." On one level, the Italian Renaissance was the rebirth of the art and learning of Classical Rome and Greece. The people of the Renaissance saw themselves as returning to the glory of Rome after a long period of cultural decline. Renaissance scholars coined the term *Dark Ages* for the centuries following the fall of Rome in 476, because they believed that the light of Roman art and learning had been completely extinguished.

Modern historians no longer view the early Middle Ages as "dark," because we now understand that the light of Roman culture never disappeared completely. Even the Germanic tribes who conquered Rome adopted Roman customs, laws, and cultural ideas. However, it is true that the light of culture burned dimly in the early Middle Ages. Latin learning was kept alive by monks, but as the years passed, many original manuscripts were lost, and newer manuscripts—copied painstakingly by hand—often contained errors. The Latin language changed, from the pure clarity of Classical Latin to the more practical Medieval Latin, which included words from other languages. The knowledge of Greek disappeared almost completely, and Greek philosophers were known only through poor Latin translations.

All of western Europe experienced this cultural decline. But Italy emerged from it earlier than the rest of the continent, and the Italian people led the way toward a new, shining light of art and learning. There are many reasons why Italy was the cradle of the Renaissance, but we can sum up most of these reasons in four words: history, geography, wealth, and freedom.

THE GLORY OF ROME AND THE CROSSROADS OF THE MEDITERRANEAN

Long after the fall of Rome, the great achievements of the Roman Empire—buildings, statues, and monuments—dotted the Italian landscape, confronting the Italian people like silent, crumbling reminders of former glory. They were almost like old friends or relatives: taken for granted, perhaps, but always there. Many Roman manuscripts still existed, too—collecting dust in monastery libraries, ignored by the

Christian monks as "pagan" writing. More than eight centuries after the fall of Rome, the rediscovery of these original manuscripts and the renewed appreciation of Roman art and architecture led to the explosion of learning and culture that we call the Renaissance.

The glory of Rome provided the inspiration for the Italian Renaissance, but the Renaissance was much more than the rebirth of old ideas. It was the development of these ideas to new heights of greatness. Why did this extraordinary development occur in Italy during the period from around 1300 to 1550? To answer this question, we must look at Italy in the late Middle Ages, just before the dawn of the Renaissance. And the best place to start is with the geography of the Italian peninsula.

The boot of Italy stretches some 700 miles from the Alps to the heart of the Mediterranean Sea. It was the natural route of travel from Europe to the eastern Mediterranean, where the Byzantine and Islamic empires enjoyed a level of wealth and culture not found in western Europe. Beginning with the first Crusade in 1096 A.D., wave after wave of European adventurers passed through Italy on their way to the Middle East. Although the Crusades were fought for religious and economic reasons, they also became a sort of "wake-up call," a reminder that the flame of learning and culture was still burning. Those who returned from the Crusades—nobles and commoners alike—had a new appreciation of beauty, luxury, and learning. And the door through which the Crusaders passed was Italy.

The combination of history and geography also brought a different kind of traveler to the Italian peninsula. Because of its central location in the Mediterranean Sea and its pleasant climate, Italy was very tempting to foreign invaders, and its history as the heart of the Roman Empire exerted a strong, almost mystical appeal to ambitious conquerors who hoped to form empires of their own. Between the fall of the Roman Empire and the beginning of the Renaissance, a long parade of foreign invaders attempted to control the Italian peninsula: Byzantines, Arabs, and Normans in the south; Germanic tribes and the Holy Roman Empire in the north. Although none of these invaders conquered the entire peninsula, they each brought their own cultural ideas, further stimulating the already rich culture of Italy.

This illuminated manuscript depicts Marco Polo sailing from Venice in 1271, at the beginning of his famous journey to China. During the Middle Ages, Italy was the starting point for many journeys that brought Europeans into contact with other civilizations, but Marco Polo traveled farther than most. (The Bodleian Library, Oxford, Ms. Bodl. 264, fol. 218r)

Of all the foreign invaders, the most powerful was the Holy Roman Empire. As its name suggests, the empire was an attempt to reunite Europe as it had once been united under the Roman Empire. The "Holy" part of the name reflected the idea that the pope was the spiritual leader of the Christian world, while the emperor was the temporal (nonspiritual) leader and defender of the Church. In reality, the pope and the emperor were often in bitter conflict over questions of authority.

By the late Middle Ages, the crown of the Holy Roman Empire had passed to a series of kings in Germany. Despite its great power in northern Europe, the Holy Roman Empire was never able to exert complete control over Italy. Once again, geography played an important role: Italy is a long way from Germany, separated by the rugged Alps. Even more important, however, was the conflict between the pope and the emperor. The late Middle Ages marked the period of greatest power for the pope and the Church. Since the papacy was centered in Rome, the power of the pope made it difficult for the emperor to gain control over Italy. And this lack of central control led directly to the next important ingredient in the making of the Renaissance: the wealth and independence of the Italian city-states.

THE RISE OF THE CITY-STATES

Although we have been discussing Italy and the Italian people, there was no nation called Italy during the Renaissance. In fact, Italy as we know it today did not exist until the second half of the 19th century. At the beginning of the Renaissance, the Italian peninsula was a land of independent cities. Each city made its own laws, hired its own armies, and collected taxes from the surrounding countryside.

These independent cities and the land they controlled are called *city-states,* but they were not states in the same way that Kansas or California are states. The 50 states of the United States are independent in many ways, yet they all function together under the federal government in Washington, D.C. Renaissance Italy had no federal government—no president, Congress, or Supreme Court. In the north, the weak rule of the emperor left the cities to their own devices in the late Middle Ages, and by the Renaissance, imperial rule was nothing but a memory. In the central peninsula, the pope claimed power over a large area called the Papal States, but it wasn't until the late Renaissance that this claim approached reality. Southern Italy also developed, but it was ruled as a feudal monarchy under foreign control throughout the Renaissance.

The first Italian city to emerge as an independent power was Venice, located on the Adriatic Sea in the northeastern corner of the peninsula. By 1000 A.D., Venice had developed a strong economy as a sea power in the eastern Mediterranean, carrying goods back and forth between Europe and the Byzantine Empire. The Crusades further enriched the economy, as Venetian ships transported the Crusaders and Venetian merchants took advantage of new trade opportunities in the Middle East. The Crusades also brought wealth to the other side of the Italian peninsula, where Genoa and Pisa emerged as independent sea powers.

The wealth of Venice, Genoa, and Pisa led to a growing economy throughout northern Italy. Among the next cities to emerge were Florence and Milan, two inland cities with excellent locations for trading and manufacturing. If Italy was the crossroads of the Mediterranean, Florence was the crossroads of Italy—located on the routes from Venice to Genoa and from Rome to northern Italy. Milan was located on the route to northern Europe.

The Italian city-states had achieved substantial wealth and independence by the mid-13th century, but the death of Emperor Frederick II in 1250 marked a clear turning point that led directly to the Renaissance. Of all the Holy Roman Emperors, Frederick was the most Italian and the most interested in ruling a united Italy. A brilliant, educated tyrant whom his admirers called "the wonder of the world," he ruled from Palermo in Sicily—an island located off the coast of southern Italy—and made many important contributions to Italian culture. But his strength and ambition represented the last great threat to the freedom of the city-states. After his death, the Holy Roman Empire continued to exist in Germany, but it was no longer an important Italian power.

During the reign of Frederick and in the chaotic years following his death, the long-simmering conflict between pope and emperor exploded into open warfare. The supporters of the pope, called Guelphs, battled the supporters of the emperor, called Ghibellines, littering the city streets and countryside with corpses. The Guelph-Ghibelline rivalry created an atmosphere of violence and division in the city-states that continued into the Renaissance period, long after the original conflict between the pope and the emperor had faded. Yet amid the hatred and bloodshed, the economic boom continued, aided by new growth north of the Alps.

By 1250, the rest of Europe was emerging from the cultural and economic decline of the Middle Ages. Most of the cities and towns of modern Europe were settled, and the population of the continent was around 70 million and growing steadily. With the end of imperial control and the emergence of new European markets, the merchant cities of Italy achieved an extraordinary level of wealth and power. By the mid-13th century, Florence was the center of European banking, and wealthy Florentine bankers insured the valuable cargoes of Venetian and Genoese ships. The gold florin, a coin first minted in Florence in 1252, became the standard European currency. After the land-based economy of the Middle Ages, the Italian city-states were developing a capitalistic economy based on money.

All this wealth stimulated the growth of the city populations. Florence is the most striking example. Along with its leadership in banking and insurance, Florence was the center of European wool manufacturing, and the wool industry drew thousands of workers from the surrounding countryside into the city. By 1200, the population of Florence was around 50,000. Then during the economic growth of the 13th century, the population doubled to almost 100,000, making it the largest city in Europe. Venice, Milan, and Genoa also had populations approaching 100,000, while Bologna and Palermo had populations approaching 50,000. By the year 1300, there were a total of 23 Italian cities with a population of 20,000 or more. These were not large cities by modern standards, but they were bustling centers of commerce and culture.

The development of the Italian city-states led to the cultural achievements of the Renaissance. For an individual, it's not necessary to be rich or independent or live in a big city to create great art or think of brilliant ideas. But for an entire city or group of cities to reach the heights of artistic and intellectual achievement, there must be money to support public art, independence to allow each city to develop its own artistic path, and a stimulating atmosphere where artists and thinkers can share ideas. This was the situation in northern Italy at the dawn of the Renaissance.

DEMOCRACY AND HUMANISM

During the 12th century, the cities of northern Italy developed a form of democratic government called a *commune.* The communes were not true democracies because the right to vote was generally limited to the men of wealthy families. And by the beginning of the Renaissance, many communes had fallen under the rule of a single man or a single family. Yet, despite their limitations, the communes produced a new level of discussion and participation in public life, creating a larger group of active, educated citizens.

At first the old noble class controlled the communes, but during the 13th century, most communes limited the rights of the nobility, and a new class took power: the *popolo,* which means the "people." The popolo was usually dominated by merchants and businessmen, who might be considered the upper middle class today, but there was also a strong lower middle class of craftsmen and artisans. And as the cities continued to develop, a new class of educated professionals emerged—what might be called the "middle" middle class.

The existence of this large, complex middle class offered new opportunities to change one's social and economic status; and social and economic freedom were essential to the development of Renaissance genius. A simple herdsman named Giotto became the most influential painter of the early Renaissance. An illegitimate middle-class child named Leonardo da Vinci became a brilliant painter and inventor, courted by dukes and kings. An aristocrat named Michelangelo Buonarroti stepped down in social class to become perhaps the greatest artist the world has ever known.

The wealth and independence of the city-states, the limited democracy of the communes, and the rise of the middle class all contributed to the development of the Renaissance. But the explosion of art and learning would never have occurred without a final freedom: the freedom of ideas. During the Middle Ages, brilliant thinkers such as Thomas Aquinas worked strictly within the framework of the Church, and medieval art was created to decorate churches and represent religious ideas. This religious emphasis reflected the belief that earthly life was a rehearsal for eternity—a difficult and rather unpleasant test by which human beings earned the joy of heaven or condemned themselves to the suffering of purgatory or hell.

The Renaissance was marked by a different view of life, a philosophy that became known as *humanism.* Renaissance humanists did not give up their faith in God or the Church. But they began to see that human beings could achieve great things in this world, that art and ideas are valuable for their own sake. In a sense, humanists discovered the full potential of the human race. Ironically, this breakthrough began with the study of law.

As the Italian city-states grew in wealth and population, there was a new concern with legal documents: business contracts, city charters, and laws. This required a new educated class of administrators, judges, lawyers, and notaries. At first, legal scholars studied Roman law as set down by a Christian emperor named Justinian in the sixth century A.D. But as they delved into ancient manuscripts, they went further back, to the writings of "pagan" Romans such as Cicero and Seneca. The secular (nonreligious) writings of the ancient Romans helped free the thinkers of the Renaissance from the structure of the Church.

The first flowering of humanism occurred during the late 13th century in the cities of northern Italy, especially Padua and Verona. There, scholars began to study and discuss classical poetry and history, as well as legal writing. Historian John R. Hale describes the excitement of this new classical research:

> They were searching in libraries for forgotten manuscripts and reading them with scholarly zest . . . concerned with establishing the correct words of a text and attributing them to the right author. This . . . gave the Renaissance a firsthand knowledge of what the ancients had actually said, and enabled it to speak with them directly, across the centuries.
>
> It is difficult to imagine the excitement that attended this unearthing of new and purer texts, this tuning in on voices that spoke with such joy and conviction about the noblest, most triumphant age that Italy has ever known. . . . The Italian humanists were discovering their own ancestors, finding buried treasure in their own house.

The early humanists did not call their philosophy humanism; they called it the *new learning,* an interesting term since it was really the rediscovery of old learning. But under any name, it was this new learning and new freedom—combined with the wealth and independence of the Italian city-states—that led to the dawn of the Renaissance.

CHAPTER 1 NOTE

p. 9   "They were searching . . ." John R. Hale. *Renaissance,* Great Ages of Man (New York: Time-Life Books, 1965), p. 16.

THE FOURTEENTH CENTURY:

Early Renaissance and Black Death

In 1302 a nobleman named Dante Alighieri was banished from the city of Florence—condemned to death by fire if he ever returned. Along with other leaders of a political party called the White Guelphs, Dante had found himself on the losing side of the old struggle between the pope and the emperor. Ironically, Dante's Guelphs had originally supported the pope, but in Florence the Guelphs split into two factions: the Whites resisted the efforts of Pope Boniface VIII to expand his power in the earthly world, while the Blacks supported Boniface. Boniface and the Blacks won the battle, but history shows us that Dante won the war.

During his years of wandering, Dante composed a long poem entitled *Commedia,* which we call *The Divine Comedy.* This poem tells the story of Dante's imaginary journey through hell, purgatory, and heaven. Scholars consider *The Divine Comedy* to be the crowning glory of medieval literature; however, Dante's great poem was also the beginning of something new, something essential for the Italian Renaissance. For with *The Divine Comedy,* Dante almost single-handedly invented the Italian language.

Before Dante, intellectuals wrote and carried on scholarly conversations in Latin, which they considered the only language worthy of expressing serious ideas. Middle-class people, who had to read and write for business purposes, generally used the dialect of their particular region. This created problems on both levels. On the one hand, Latin was a language of books rather than everyday life, a "dead" language not well-suited for expressing new ideas. On the other hand, there were too many regional dialects in Italy, and most of these dialects were rough and poorly formed, without a clear structure. In *The Divine Comedy,* Dante used the Tuscan dialect spoken in Florence, but refined it with aspects of Latin and other languages into a beautiful language suitable for both everyday conversation and brilliant literary expression. Although scholars continued to write in Latin, it was Dante's Italian that evolved into the language of the Renaissance.

By the time that Dante left Florence, an artist named Giotto had begun to establish a reputation as the greatest painter of his age. We know little of Giotto's early life, but according to legend he was a goatherd who developed his painter's eye by observing the Tuscan countryside. During the early 14th century, Giotto's fame spread throughout the Italian peninsula. Although his technique was primitive compared to that of later Renaissance artists, he brought a startling power and emotion to painting that marks a major development from the flat, rigid style of the Middle Ages.

Art historians generally look at Giotto as the beginning of Renaissance painting, while literary scholars consider Dante as the height of medieval literature. But from a purely historical point of view, these two brilliant men of Florence represent the beginning of a new age, the first hints of the Italian Renaissance.

THE AGE OF THE SIGNORI AND CONDOTTIERI

In *The Divine Comedy,* Dante places his old enemy Pope Boniface VIII in hell. We leave this moral judgment to Dante. But it's true that Boniface, who reigned from 1294 to 1303, was one of the most politically ambitious and corrupt popes of the time, and in the end his ambitions led to the downfall of the papacy. When King Philip IV of France taxed the clergy to pay for a war with England, Boniface excommunicated him and wrote a papal bull (an official pronouncement) asserting the pope's absolute authority in both spiritual *and* worldly matters. In retaliation, Philip ordered soldiers to capture Boniface, and though the aged pope was never actually imprisoned, he died a few weeks later. This marked a turning point, shifting control of the papacy from Italy to France. In 1305 the French Pope Clement V was crowned in Lyons, France instead of in Rome. Four years later, Clement officially moved the papacy to the French city of Avignon, where it remained for almost 70 years.

With the pope out of Italy, the Holy Roman Emperor Henry VII attempted to reestablish control in 1310. Some idealistic patriots, including Dante, welcomed him with open arms—hoping that a strong emperor might unite all of Italy—but most Italians responded less enthusiastically. Henry resorted to war, but his death in 1313 ended imperial ambitions until an equally unsuccessful invasion by Emperor Lewis IV in 1327–1330. Robert of Anjou, the French ruler of southern Italy, helped repel both these invasions and gained some power in the north, but he was no more successful at controlling Italy than the Holy Roman Emperors had been. Throughout the 14th century, the Italian city-states were free to chart their own destiny.

Looking back from our perspective in the modern world, it's easy to imagine that this freedom might have led to an age of great democracy. But in fact, it had the opposite result. Italian towns of the early 14th century were dangerous, chaotic places. The ruling class of bankers and merchants, along with the old noble class, fought among themselves for control of the growing wealth. At the same time, the middle class of artisans and craftsmen fought for greater power in city government, and the huge lower class of poor workers—who had no power at all—added to the unrest.

Faced with this explosive, often violent situation, many city-states turned to political strongmen called *signori*. The rise of the signori had begun in the late 13th century, but it gained momentum throughout the 14th century as city after city turned over control of their once-democratic communes to a single man—with the hope that he could keep the peace. Only Venice in the north and the Tuscan cities of

Florence, Siena, Lucca, and Pisa maintained a form of democracy through most of this period, with power generally exercised by a small group of wealthy businessmen.

Whether ruled by tyrants or elected officials, the city-states spent much of the century battling for power and position, with the bigger cities gradually absorbing their weaker neighbors. This was the age of the *condottieri*—mercenary soldier-captains who roamed the countryside, selling the services of their armies to the highest bidder. When they weren't fighting under contract, the mercenary armies attacked travelers and preyed on ordinary citizens, demanding "protection money" in a manner similar to 20th-century gangsters.

It was a frightening and bloody age. Yet, amid the warfare and chaos, a poet took center stage.

PETRARCH, THE FIRST RENAISSANCE MAN

Francesco Petrarch was born in 1304, the son of a lawyer who had been banished from Florence with Dante in the Guelph conflict. Petrarch's father later found a position with the papal court in Avignon, and it was there that young Francesco grew to manhood. After studying law at the University of Bologna, Petrarch returned to Avignon in 1326, and the following year, while attending an early-morning church service, he first glimpsed a young married woman named Laura who became the ideal, unattainable love of his life. At least that's the story; some scholars doubt that Laura ever existed. But whether real or imagined, Laura inspired Petrarch to write poems in beautiful, flowing Italian that ushered in a new age of poetry and gained their author great fame in Italian society.

Petrarch also wrote prolifically in Latin: philosophy, collections of ancient learning, a guidebook to the Holy Land, epic poetry, detailed letters, and a "secret book" in which he analyzed his own life in a dialogue with Saint Augustine. Powerfully drawn to the beauties of nature, he traveled throughout Europe and climbed a mountain in the Alps just for the view. He rediscovered Latin manuscripts and thought of classical writers like Cicero and Virgil as old friends. Petrarch disdained the world around him—full of war, tyranny, greed, and ignorance—yet he lived the life of the mind passionately and completely. His writings show us a human being very much aware of *being* a human being—always sensible to the passage of time and the wonderful delicacy of life:

> I . . . was thinking of what to say next, and as my habit is, I was pricking the paper idly with my pen. And I thought how, between one dip of the pen and the next, time goes on, and I hurry, drive myself, with speed toward death. We are always dying, I while I write, you while you read, and others while they listen or stop their ears, they are all dying.

On one level this may seem a gloomy reflection on death; yet it is really a crystal clear and very modern view of life itself. Petrarch has been called the first great humanist scholar, the first modern writer, and indeed the first modern man. He influenced other writers of the time, notably Giovanni Boccaccio, who popularized Italian prose much as Petrarch popularized Italian poetry. "Petrarch had none of Dante's gigantic vision," writes historian John Julius Norwich, "but his more slender genius led the way forward to a fresh uncluttered outlook."

On April 8, 1341, the people of Rome revived an ancient Roman custom and crowned Petrarch poet laureate on the Roman Capitol. Symbolically, this ceremony marks the high point of the early artistic Renaissance. For centuries, popes and emperors had been crowned in the Eternal City; now the pope and the emperor were gone, and a poet wore the crown.

Six years later, in May 1347, another ancient Roman ceremony took place on the Capitol. Cola di Rienzo, son of a Roman washerwoman, was invested with the title Tribune of the Roman Republic and given absolute dictatorial powers. Cola had led a popular uprising against the aristocracy, preaching a return to the glorious days of Rome. Petrarch was one of Cola's greatest supporters, and in many ways Cola was attempting to do in politics what Petrarch was doing in literature. But politics is a more dangerous business.

By December of that year, Cola had alienated his supporters—as well as the other Italian city-states—and was driven into exile. When he returned in 1354, wearing Roman-style armor and holding the banner of ancient Rome, the mob turned against him. In the midst of a riot, he was stabbed to death and hung by his feet in a public square.

"Where are these good Romans?" Cola had asked. "Where is their perfect justice? . . . If only I could have lived in their day."

ECONOMIC COLLAPSE AND THE BLACK DEATH

The economic boom of the late Middle Ages continued into the early 14th century. Some historians believe that the economy began to slow down around 1320, but in 1330, there were still 80 large banks in Florence, and one of these—the Bardi—had branches, not only throughout Italy, but in foreign cities from London to Constantinople. By 1341, however—the year Petrarch was crowned poet laureate—the economic tide had clearly begun to turn.

The rapid growth of city populations, combined with poor farming practices, bad weather, and marauding mercenary armies in the countryside, resulted in four major famines from 1339 to 1375. The situation worsened during the 1340s when King Edward III of England refused to pay back huge sums of money he had borrowed from the banking houses of Florence to finance a war against France. In quick succession, the once-powerful Florentine banks collapsed, and smaller businesses soon followed.

It was in this atmosphere of famine and economic depression that the Black Death came to Italy. Thought to be a combination of three forms of bacterial plague (bubonic, pneumonic, and septicemic), the devastating epidemic originated in India and soon spread to the Middle East and the Crimea. In October 1347, Genoese ships brought the plague to the island of Sicily, and by early 1348, it had spread through the coastal cities of Genoa, Pisa, and Venice. That spring, it ravaged Florence and Rome.

It's estimated that the Black Death killed one third of the people of Europe between 1347 and 1351. The Italian city-states, with their large populations crowded behind city walls, suffered even more than the rest of Europe. Accounts of the time suggested that 70 percent of the Italian population died. This figure is too high for the country as a whole, but in the major cities the death toll was probably over 50 percent. The plague touched everyone: rich and poor, commoner and noble, farmer and townsperson. Among the victims was Petrarch's beloved Laura—if there ever was a Laura.

BOCCACCIO'S *DECAMERON:*
PROSE AND THE PLAGUE

Giovanni Boccaccio was born in Tuscany in 1313, the illegitimate son of a middle-class merchant. As a young man, he enjoyed living in the southern Italian city of Naples, but he returned to Florence in 1341 and lived there for most of his life, establishing himself—along with his friend and mentor, Petrarch—as one of the two great writers of the early Italian Renaissance.

Like Petrarch, Boccaccio wrote philosophical works in Latin and rediscovered the thought and writing of the classical age. He had a special interest in ancient Greek, almost completely unknown in his time, and employed an eccentric, incompetent Greek scholar to make one of the first—and worst—translations of Homer into Latin. But though his contributions to humanist philosophy and classical scholarship were important, Boccaccio is best known for his extraordinary writing in Italian prose, developing a realistic, bawdy style unlike anything that had been written before.

Boccaccio's most famous prose work is the *Decameron,* a collection of 100 stories told by 10 people in 10 days. Many of these stories involve romantic adventures, and Boccaccio tells them with an openness that was shocking for his time. But the people of the Renaissance read them as avidly as people today read a popular novel.

This wholesale death produced fundamental changes in Italian society. The political and economic situation, already falling apart before the plague, descended into chaos and anarchy. On a more personal level, the survivors faced psychological depression and frightening uncertainty. "No one wept for the dead," wrote one survivor, "because everyone expected death himself." The plague returned with horrible regularity several times over the next 50 years, making recovery slow and difficult. If we consider the paintings of

The *Decameron* begins in Florence during the Black Death of 1348, when seven young ladies and three young men meet in a church and decide to travel to the countryside to escape the sickness. In setting the stage, Boccaccio describes the Black Death with the same realism that he employs in the stories themselves. His words carry through the ages to give us a glimpse of the horrible time of the plague:

> . . . it began both in men and women with certain swellings in the groin or under the armpit. They grew to the size of a small apple or an egg, more or less, and were vulgarly called tumors. In a short space of time these spread from the two parts named all over the body. Soon after this the symptoms changed and black or purple spots appeared on the arms or thighs or any other part of the body, sometimes a few large ones, sometimes many little ones. These spots were a certain sign of death. . . .
>
> . . . So violent was the malignancy of this plague that it was communicated, not only from one man to another, but from the garments of a sick or dead man to animals of another species. . . . One day among other occasions I saw with my own eyes . . . the rags left lying in the street of a poor man who had died of the plague; two pigs came along and, as their habit is, turned the clothes over with their snouts and then munched at them, with the result that they both fell dead almost at once on the rags, as if they had been poisoned.

Giotto and the writings of Petrarch and Boccaccio to be an early artistic Renaissance, then in the later 14th century the Renaissance was put on hold.

In 1377 Pope Gregory IX returned to Rome, concerned by a powerful wave of anti-papal feeling that had swept through the Italian cities. When Gregory died the following year, the Roman people insisted that an Italian be elected pope and surrounded the building where the cardinals gathered to vote. Faced with the threat

The Dance of Death—which personified death as a dancing partner for the living—was a popular myth in the late Middle Ages, but the Black Death of 1348 made it more real than ever before. (From *La Grande Danse Macabre*, Paris, 1862; Library of Congress)

of violence, the cardinals chose the Italian Pope Urban VI, but a group of French cardinals later chose their own pope to rule from Avignon. This created the Great Schism, with two lines of popes, one in Rome and one in Avignon. In 1409 the Church called a council in the Italian city of Pisa to resolve the conflict—but only managed to produce a third line of popes! The Great Schism was finally resolved in 1417, although its effects lasted into the mid-15th century.

While the Great Schism raged within the Church, bloodier conflicts raged in the Italian countryside. In the atmosphere of population loss and instability that followed the Black Death, the larger city-states increased their efforts to gobble up their smaller neighbors. This territorial expansion continued well into the 15th century, and a few smaller cities maintained their independence. But the age of the Italian Renaissance was primarily defined by five great powers: Florence, Rome, Venice, Milan, and Naples.

CHAPTER 2 NOTES

p. 14   "I . . . was thinking . . ." Petrarch; quoted in Morris Bishop. "Petrarch," in *The Horizon Book of the Renaissance* (New York: American Heritage, 1961), p. 32.

p. 14   "Petrarch had none of . . ." John Julius Norwich. "Barbarians, Priests, and Communes," in *An Illustrated History of Italy,* (New York: McGraw-Hill, 1966), p. 102.

p. 15   "Where are these . . ." Cola di Rienzo; quoted in Giuliano Procacci. *History of the Italian People* (New York: Harper & Row, 1968), p. 68.

p. 16   "No one wept . . ." Agnola di Tura; quoted in "European Society 1250–1450." *The Random House Encyclopedia* (New York: Random House, 1983), p. 1103.

p. 17   "it began both in men and women . . ." *The Decameron of Giovanni Boccaccio,* trans. Richard Aldington (New York: Dell, 1962.) p. 31.

FLORENCE:

Heart of the Renaissance

Florence spreads along the banks of the Arno River, more than 50 miles from the sea, surrounded by the rolling hills and valleys of Tuscany. By the end of the 14th century, after years of famine, plague, and warfare, some 50,000 hardy souls were living behind the city walls, struggling to put their once-prosperous world back together again. This was less than half the population of the 1330s—a mere handful by the standards of modern cities. Yet from these few Florentines, their children, and their children's children arose an astonishing parade of great artists and thinkers that became the very heart of the Italian Renaissance.

Of all the major city-states, Florence had the strongest tradition of democratic rule. A century earlier, in 1293, the citizens had adopted new laws that took power from the old nobility and placed it firmly in the hands of the rising middle class. In order to hold political office, a Florentine had to belong to one of the guilds—organizations of businessmen and craftsmen, divided into seven great guilds and 14 lesser guilds. The great guilds, called the *popolo grasso* (fat people), included the wealthiest and most powerful men of the city, dominated by the cloth finishers, wool merchants, and bankers.

The lesser guilds, called the *popolo minuto* (little people), included smaller businessmen and craftsmen such as innkeepers, grocers, shoemakers, and blacksmiths. For most of the 14th century, these two factions struggled furiously to control city government, with the old conflicts between Guelphs and Ghibellines adding to the confusion.

The 21 guilds comprised only a small percentage of the population, perhaps 3,000 or 4,000 men. Women couldn't vote, slavery was legal (as long as the slaves weren't Christians), and the vast majority of Florentine men were day laborers who had no say in the government at all. Nonetheless, Florence was a model democracy of the time. The guild-member citizens assembled in the public square to pass major laws, while the head of state and chief magistrates served for only two months at a time. In theory, this made it difficult for one man to gain too much power, although men who wanted power found ways to get it. Just as important, Florentines experienced many different facets of city government as they moved from one position to another, producing a class of knowledgeable men who considered civic service an essential part of their lives.

It is not by accident that Florence and surrounding Tuscany produced the four greatest writers and artists of the early Renaissance: Dante, Giotto, Petrarch, and Boccaccio. At the same time it's typical of Florentine politics that Dante and Petrarch both lived in exile from the city. For the nobly born Dante, who had to join the druggists' guild in order to take part in city politics, the exile was forced on pain of death. For Petrarch, born during his father's exile, it became an exile of choice as he wandered from city to city looking for peace of mind and soul. During much of the 14th century, peace of any kind was hard to find in Florence.

In 1378 the wool workers and other day laborers revolted, demanding representation in the government as a guild. On one level, this revolt was part of a general European uprising of the lower class, spurred by labor shortages following the Black Death. At the same time, it was just politics as usual, because the real leaders of the rebellion were not the common workers but rather the *popolo minuto,* who used the workers as a way to gain power themselves.

The revolt of the wool workers disturbed the city's commerce, and when the wealthy *popolo grasso* regained power in 1382, they took measures to solidify their control of the city government. The already imperfect democracy of Florence became even less democratic, with power resting in the hands of a small group of very wealthy men—a "government by the few" called an oligarchy. The man who emerged as the leader of this ruling faction was a wealthy wool merchant named Maso degli Albizzi. For the next half century, the Albizzi family and their allies dominated Florentine politics, establishing a pattern of subtle yet firm individual rule that was later taken to new heights by a more famous Florentine family, the Medici.

Despite the behind-the-scenes reality of rule by the few, the Florentines maintained a fierce pride in their republican form of government, with laws, elected officials, and popular participation. This patriotism faced a difficult test when the militant despot of Milan, Gian Galeazzo Visconti, declared war on Florence in 1390. For 12 frightening years, the Florentines watched Visconti's armies and propaganda conquer city after city in Tuscany and the northern Papal States. Visconti's supporters claimed that he was waging a noble war to unify Italy, but the Florentines saw it as a life and death struggle between tyranny and freedom.

THE NEW ROMANS

From 1375 to 1406, the humanist scholar Coluccio Salutati served as chancellor of Florence, the only long-term position in Florentine government. The chancellor handled a number of important tasks, including writing public documents and diplomatic letters to foreign powers. In a sense, he provided intellectual leadership in combination with the political/economic leadership of the ruling oligarchy. During the long war with Milan, Salutati and his young protégé Leonardo Bruni rallied the Florentine people with the belief that they were the "new Romans," the true heirs to the glorious Roman Republic. Salutati's writing was so powerful that his enemy, Gian Galeazzo Visconti, once said that a public letter by Salutati was worth more than a thousand cavalry.

"Liberty is properly obedient to the laws, while tyranny is obedient to one single man who governs everything according to his caprices," Salutati wrote in one manifesto. "Tyranny equals fear; fear of the signore, of his suspicions, of his fickle motives, of his humors. . . . This is the destiny that awaits every people that Giangaleazzo [Visconti] succeeds in conquering."

Although Salutati's ringing words inspired the Florentine spirit, many citizens faced the end of the century with a sense of dread. A freezing April produced famine in 1399, and the Tuscan cities of Pisa and Siena fell to Visconti's forces. Some thought the world would end along with the century, and they wandered the countryside, wearing coarse sheets that made them look like ghosts, fasting, doing penance, and praying for deliverance. When the year 1400 arrived, it seemed that the prophets of doom weren't far from wrong. The plague returned—not as bad as the Black Death of 1348, but bad enough—and Visconti tightened his pressure on the city, cutting off trade and food supplies.

Then, in September 1402, Gian Galeazzo Visconti died suddenly of a fever. To the people of Florence it seemed as though Visconti's death was a sign from God that their republican form of government was right, that they really were the "new Romans." This feeling of patriotism and destiny continued to grow when Florence conquered the city of Pisa in 1406, giving it access to the sea. Other conquests and

Florence in a woodcut from around 1486, with the domed cathedral dominating the center of the city. (Facsimile of woodcut in Staatliche Museen, Berlin)

THE DOORS TO
THE ARTISTIC RENAISSANCE

In 1400, while Florence suffered from famine, plague, and the approaching armies of Milan, the wealthy wool merchants' guild decided to commission a set of bronze doors for the church of St. John the Baptist, called the Baptistery. St. John was the patron saint of the city, and according to legend the church had once been a Roman temple of the god Mars. Thus the Baptistery represented both the pious Christian present and the glorious Roman past. The merchants had been planning the doors for some time, but it's indicative of early Renaissance thought that they decided to commission them at a time when sickness and warfare threatened the city.

After an open competition, the guild selected six or seven artists and gave each a sum of money to complete a sample panel depicting the Biblical story of Abraham sacrificing his son Isaac. According to some stories, the entry by Lorenzo Ghiberti was narrowly chosen over the entry by Filippo Brunelleschi, while others say that the guild offered to split the commission between the two, and Brunelleschi refused to collaborate. In any event, the commission went to Ghiberti.

Lorenzo Ghiberti took 20 years to complete the Baptistery doors. At the time he began, the Florentines had only a basic knowledge of classical sculpture, but Ghiberti used this knowledge to create a series of powerful, graceful panels that seemed to trumpet a new world. In the meantime, Filippo Brunelleschi brought the new world into reality. Disgusted with the results of the competition, Brunelleschi vowed to become an architect and left Florence for Rome, accompa-

annexations followed as Florence expanded its territory to include most of Tuscany. At the same time, the Florentines held off two invasions by the king of Naples between 1408 and 1414. And when the forces of Milan again threatened its independence in 1425, Florence entered an nied by his young friend, Donatello. Together the two Florentine artists studied the ruins of ancient Roman buildings as eagerly as the humanists studied Roman writing.

For a dozen years, Brunelleschi divided his time between Florence and Rome, gradually gaining an understanding of two key "secrets" from the past: the principles of Roman architecture and the laws of mathematical perspective. Brunelleschi used his knowledge of Roman architecture and construction techniques to build the great dome of Florence's cathedral. The Florentine artist Masaccio learned perspective from Brunelleschi and used it to create powerful paintings whose figures seemed more alive than anything ever painted before. In sculpture, Brunelleschi's friend Donatello—who was only 17 when he first went to Rome—emerged as the leading figure of the age, combining classical ideals that he observed among the ruins with a new, graceful vision.

When Ghiberti finished his doors, the merchants were so pleased that they commissioned him to design another set. This time Ghiberti used the new understanding of perspective—learned from his old rival Brunelleschi—to take his work to another level. Years later, when Michelangelo saw this second set of doors, he found them so beautiful that he said they were worthy to stand at the Gates of Paradise.

Ghiberti's doors are among the finest Florentine creations of the early Renaissance. But we can't help wondering what might have happened if Brunelleschi had won the competition instead. Would he have stayed in Florence working on the doors, never venturing to explore the ruins of Rome? And if so, how would this have changed the development of the artistic Renaissance?

alliance with Venice, the other republican power, to hold off the danger from the north.

During this period, while Florence solidified its position as one of the great independent powers on the Italian peninsula, the city experienced the first brilliant accomplishments of the artistic Renaissance. (See box feature.) And the leading figure of the early Florentine Renaissance, the architect Filippo Brunelleschi, gave the city a monument to its newfound greatness: the cathedral known as *il Duomo*, the dome.

Begun during the time of Dante, the cathedral of Florence was the largest church in the Christian world. In fact, it was so large that—more than a century since the church was begun—no one had been able to build the great dome that was supposed to cover the sanctuary. After studying Roman architecture, Brunelleschi confidently claimed that he would not only build the dome but build it higher and stronger than originally planned. He proved as good as his word, beginning work in 1420 and completing the project in 1436 as the bells of Florence rang with joy. The soaring, graceful dome—larger than any other dome in the world—seemed a perfect symbol of Florence's central place in that world, so much so that homesick Florentine travelers would say they were "sick for the dome."

THE ASCENT OF THE MEDICI

In 1420, when Brunelleschi began work on the dome, Florence was still dominated by the Albizzi family. By the time the dome was completed 16 years later, a new family had taken control: the Medici. Of all the great families of the Italian Renaissance the Medici represent most completely the combination of wealth, power, and culture that made the Renaissance such an extraordinary period.

The family's rise to wealth and power began in 1397, when Giovanni di Bicci de' Medici founded the Medici Bank. He gradually built it into the dominant financial force in Florence, loaning money to a wide variety of creditors including foreign princes, the Church, and Florence itself. The Church had strict laws against usury—the practice of charging interest on loans— so the Medici had to call interest charges *discrezione* (favor or yield), pretending that interest was freely given by the borrower rather than required as part of the loan. Nonetheless, interest payments formed the heart of the Medici fortune, along with other investments in trade and manufacturing.

When Giovanni died in 1429, his son Cosimo succeeded him as head of the Medici Bank and quickly found himself embroiled in Florentine politics, a danger his father had carefully avoided. In 1433 the Albizzi oligarchy charged Cosimo with plotting to overthrow the government and—in the great tradition of Florentine politics—expelled him from the city. Only a number of well-placed bribes saved his life. The details behind Cosimo's expulsion are complex, but he represented a threat to the conservative Albizzi party, because, though Cosimo himself was a member of the *popolo grasso*, he had the strong support of the *popolo minuto*. This connection between the wealthy bankers and the middle class had begun half a century earlier, when a middle-class relative of the Medici led the wool workers in revolt.

A different sort of revolt occurred in 1434, when a new city government invited Cosimo to return from his year-long exile and the Albizzi faction was banished instead. For the next 30 years Cosimo de' Medici dominated the city on a level that the Albizzi family dreamed of but never achieved. In effect, he was a king without a crown. He held important positions in city government, including serving as the ceremonial head of state for three short two-month terms. But he held these positions no more frequently than other wealthy men; his real control was behind the scenes, where by the force of his money, diplomatic skill, and shrewd judgment he controlled everything of importance that happened in the city.

Cosimo was a serious-minded businessman who led the Medici Bank to even greater financial success, establishing branches in several European cities and making Medici money an essential ingredient in European as well as Italian politics. But Cosimo also had a genuine love of the new learning. He received a humanist education, and even learned some Greek, which was just beginning to be taught in Florence. He treasured great books, funding foreign expeditions in search of lost manuscripts and founding three libraries, including his own private collection. He commissioned translations of Plato and funded a center for Greek studies known as the Platonic Academy.

Cosimo was also a lavish patron of the arts, building many beautiful churches decorated with great art and with the Medici coat of arms— the latter to remind the Florentines who was footing the bill. He pioneered in taking art out of the Church, showing a surprisingly modern and sophisticated taste for a tough-minded businessman. When he built his family home, the Palazzo Medici, he commissioned the sculptor Donatello to create a statue of David—not the older King

David usually represented in medieval art, but a youthful David unfettered by clothing, the first freestanding nude figure since the days of ancient Rome.

Cosimo's greatest accomplishment, however, was in the field of diplomacy, where he tried to provide a climate of political stability in which his business enterprises could flourish. In 1454 he was instrumental in creating the Peace of Lodi, an agreement whereby the five major powers accepted their current borders. This agreement lasted for 40 years, and though broken several times, it was the closest thing to peace that Italy experienced during the Renaissance. Cosimo's key diplomatic move was the decision to support the new ruler of Milan, Francesco Sforza, against Florence's old ally, Venice. The move was unpopular in Florence, whose older citizens still remembered the aggression of Milan's Visconti dynasty, but it changed the existing balance of power and led directly to the peace.

When Cosimo died in 1464, his role as the leading citizen of Florence was inherited by his son Piero. This stirred resentment in the city—for only the son of a king or prince inherits his position—and there were attempts to end Medici rule. But by 1466, the family was more firmly in power than ever. Although Piero continued Cosimo's patronage of the arts, he was bedridden during much of his rule, racked by pain from gout. He died five years after his father, and this time power passed smoothly to Piero's son, Lorenzo.

After Cosimo's death, the Florentines had honored him with the title of *Pater Patriæ*, "Father of the State." They called Piero *il Gottoso*, "the Gouty." But they gave Lorenzo the finest title of all: *il Magnifico*, "the Magnificent."

FLORENCE UNDER LORENZO THE MAGNIFICENT

Lorenzo was not quite 21 when his father died. Brilliant, sensitive, and superbly educated, he had already established himself as an extraordinary young man. He had grown up watching his grandfather Cosimo lead the city with a firm but delicate hand, and his invalid father Piero had sent him on an important diplomatic mission to the pope. So it was not surprising that the leaders of Florence asked him to take control. Later in his life, Lorenzo described the meeting, revealing much about his own character and the way that the Medici viewed their role in the city:

Two days after the death of my father, although I, Lorenzo, was very young, being only in my twenty-first year, the principal men of the city came to our house to condole on our loss and encourage me to take on myself the care of the city and the state, as my father and grandfather had done. This proposal being contrary to the instincts of my youthful age and considering that the burden and danger were great, I consented unwillingly, but I did so to protect our friends and our property, for it fares ill in Florence with anyone who possesses great wealth without any control of the government.

At first Lorenzo ruled easily, with little resistance from the Florentines. His father Piero had weathered the great storm of succession, and the people were willing to accept Lorenzo as their natural leader. In many ways they viewed him as a prince, and Lorenzo played the role with an unusual combination of royal style and republican humility. He married a Roman noblewoman and staged spectacles and lavish celebrations; yet he tipped his hat to ordinary citizens in the streets, and unlike other Medicis before him, refused any official role in the city government. He brought the Medici tradition of learning and artistic patronage to new levels, surrounding himself with humanist scholars and discussing Greek philosophy with them as an equal. He was an accomplished poet himself, and his writing in Italian helped elevate popular and scholarly respect for the "everyday" language. One of Lorenzo's verses seems to sum up the happy early years of his rule:

How passing fair is youth,
Forever fleeting away;
Who happy would be, let him be;
Of tomorrow who can say?

Lorenzo's "passing fair youth" as ruler of Florence ended in 1478, when an old Florentine family, the Pazzi, entered into a conspiracy with Pope Sixtus IV to overthrow the Medici. The conspirators struck in the great cathedral on Easter Sunday, when a priest stabbed Lorenzo's younger brother Giuliano, and one of the Pazzi family finished the murder with 18 dagger blows. Lorenzo himself escaped with a cut on the neck and hid behind the locked door of the sacristy. When the Pazzi tried to rally the people to their cause, the Florentines threw their support wholeheartedly behind the Medici. They hung the leaders of the plot and combed the city for anyone suspected in the conspiracy. In all, some 270 suspects were killed and others were banished or imprisoned. Even the Pazzi name was wiped out.

In retaliation, Sixtus excommunicated Lorenzo and the entire Florentine state. (Excommunication officially cuts off participation in the Church.) When the Florentine clergy excommunicated him right back, Sixtus declared war, supported by King Ferrante of Naples, whose troops invaded Tuscany. As the tide of battle turned against Florence, Lorenzo offered to give himself up rather than subject his people to further hardships. But the Florentine government refused to allow him to become the scapegoat. Nonetheless, Lorenzo slipped away and, in a stunning feat of personal diplomacy, sailed to Naples where he presented himself to the king. Ferrante was so impressed by Lorenzo's bravery and persuasive intelligence that he agreed to give up the war, leaving Pope Sixtus without an army. In time, the pope made peace as well.

The Pazzi Conspiracy and the murder of his beloved brother Giuliano changed Lorenzo. He became more of a tyrant, dissolving the old Florentine government and replacing it with a special council that was responsible only to him. Although many grumbled over his totalitarian rule, his strong hand in Florence gave him an equally strong hand in maintaining the precarious balance of power on the Italian peninsula. At the same time, Lorenzo devoted even greater money and attention to the arts, bringing Florence to the heights of the artistic Renaissance. This was the age of the brilliant humanist Pico della Mirandola, the exquisite painter Botticelli, the young genius Leonardo da Vinci, and the younger genius Michelangelo, whom Lorenzo raised in his own household along with his children.

Lorenzo died at the age of 43 in 1492, the same year that another great Italian, Christopher Columbus, stumbled upon a New World. For Florence, his death marked the beginning of the end of the Renaissance. To some extent this was Lorenzo's fault, for he was more interested in diplomacy and culture than in banking, and the Medici Bank—which had been the backbone of Florentine wealth—declined during his tenure. But there were other forces working in the world as well.

Lorenzo the Magnificent in a terra cotta bust by his favorite sculptor, Verrocchio—who taught Leonardo da Vinci and also influenced Michelangelo. (Andrea del Verrocchio, *Lorenzo de' Medici*, Samuel H. Kress collection, ©1994 National Gallery of Art, Washington)

One of these forces was a Dominican monk named Girolamo Savonarola, who preached fiery sermons against the excesses of Lorenzo and the Florentine people. He advocated a return to democracy and Christian piety. It is said that as Lorenzo lay dying the monk demanded the restoration of Florentine democracy as the price of salvation. When Pope Innocent VIII died shortly after Lorenzo, to be replaced by the incredibly corrupt Rodrigo Borgia (Alexander VI), Savonarola preached against the pope as well, calling for a foreign "scourge of God" to come and set Italy back on the road of righteousness.

In October 1494, the foreign scourge arrived in the armies of King Charles VIII of France, who crossed the Alps to press his claims on the throne of Naples. As the troops approached Florence, Lorenzo's son Piero went out to meet Charles and meekly offered the use of several Tuscan strongholds and an enormous loan of 200,000 ducats. When Piero returned and told the Florentine leaders what he had done, the people rose up against him and drove him from the city. After the French moved on to Rome, Savonarola took control of Florence and began an intense period of religious revival and democratic reform. In 1497, during the normally festive time of Carnival, the religious leader had a huge pyramid of wood built in the central plaza and demanded that the Florentines place all their "vanities" onto the structure: their nonreligious books and art work, their games and playing cards, their hairpieces and mirrors. Then he set it on fire—the bonfire of the vanities.

By the following year, the people of Florence had had enough of religious revival, and Savonarola himself was burned in the same public square. But even as the ashes cooled, the Florentines knew that their world had changed. The small city-state could not resist the enormous power of the new nation-states like France. And spurred on by Savonarola, they had turned their backs on the glorious art and learning that had made their city great. Even Savonarola's promise of renewed Christianity and democracy had ended in failure. For Florence, the Renaissance was over. Now the great artists and thinkers turned their eyes toward Rome and the cities of the North.

CHAPTER 3 NOTES

p. 23   "Liberty is properly . . ." Coluccio Salutati; quoted in Vincent Cronin. *The Florentine Renaissance* (New York: E. P. Dutton, 1967), pp. 41-42.

p. 29   "Two days after . . ." Lorenzo de' Medici; quoted in Ralph Roeder. "Lorenzo de' Medici," in *The Horizon Book*, p. 148.

p. 29   "How passing fair . . ." Lorenzo de' Medici; ibid. quoted in Roeder. p. 148.

ROME:

Church and State

During the mid-14th century, Rome was one of the strangest, saddest cities in Italy. Like other Italian cities, it suffered from the Black Death, but even before the plague, it had fallen into a state of decline. With the papacy in Avignon, the vast official bureaucracy of the Church had deserted the city, leaving it a relatively small provincial town of perhaps 20,000 people. Cows grazed among the ruins of the ancient Roman Forum, and noble families fought for control of what little economic activity remained. Unlike Florence, Rome had no manufacturing or important trade activities, and most of its income depended on religious pilgrims who came to the Holy City in search of special forgiveness for their sins, called indulgences.

In the other regions of the Papal States the situation was even worse. Tyrants took over the cities, threw out the papal representative, and ruled unchallenged. These despots were often supported by the people at first, for the pope had taxed the cities heavily and interfered in their affairs. But in the absence of central authority, the rule of the cities became more and more oppressive. In the countryside, the nobles fought among themselves and terrorized the peasants, with roving bandits and mercenary armies adding to the dangers.

The rise of Cola di Rienzo in the 1340s offered the Roman people a brief moment of excitement and hope, as he promised a return to the glories of the Roman Republic. But when Rienzo's promises proved as empty as the papal throne, the mob turned against him, driving him from the city in late 1347 and murdering him when he returned in 1354.

The man who accompanied Rienzo on his return to Rome fared better. Pope Innocent VI had sent Spanish cardinal Gil Albornoz on a special mission to bring the Papal States under control. Trained as a soldier, Cardinal Albornoz used a combination of warfare and diplomacy to force the unruly nobles and petty tyrants to accept papal rule. After Albornoz's death in 1367, the work was carried on by French cardinals who lacked his diplomatic skills and managed to alienate most of Italy. More than 80 towns expelled their papal garrisons, and Florence fought the papacy in the so-called War of the Eight Saints from 1375 to 1378. (The "saints" were the Florentine leaders.)

Disturbed by this anti-papal feeling, Pope Gregory XI returned to Rome in January 1377, welcomed by cheering crowds. The cheers proved premature when Gregory died the following year, and the Church was split by the Great Schism (1378–1417), with one line of popes in Rome and another line of popes in Avignon. For a time, a third line of popes in Pisa made the situation even more confusing. The Great Schism severely weakened the authority of the papacy, plunging Rome and the Papal States back into anarchy and chaos. (For more on Cola di Rienzo and the Great Schism, see Chapter 2.)

RISING FROM THE RUINS

The Great Schism officially ended with the reign of Pope Martin V from 1417 to 1431. Born into the Roman noble family of the Colonna, Martin was a powerful personality who reorganized the Church bureaucracy (called the Roman Curia) and worked to stop the violent anarchy that was destroying his native city. But despite his efforts, Rome remained a dangerous place for the popes. Martin himself did not spend his whole reign in the city, and his successor, Eugenius IV (1431–47), was forced to flee from Rome disguised as a monk, sailing down the Tiber River in a rowboat.

Eugenius moved the papal court to Florence, where he enjoyed the company of the humanists and artists. He left the hard task of

Rome in a pre-16th-century woodcut; the old St. Peter's basilica and the buildings of the Vatican are in the upper right, across the Tiber River from the city. (USZ62-34825, Schreiber Collection, Library of Congress)

controlling Rome in the hands of a ruthless bishop named Vitelleschi, who burned cities, executed rebellious nobles, and ended up being poisoned to death himself—possibly through Eugenius's efforts. Eugenius also faced conflict within the Church, and in 1439 a group of cardinals elected an opposing pope, the last of the "antipopes." However, despite his problems in Rome and in the Church, Eugenius made an important diplomatic move when he recognized the claims of the Spanish royal family of Aragon to the throne of Naples. This strained relations with his friends in Florence, but Naples became a staunch ally of the papacy, providing the pope with much-needed military support.

During Eugenius's troubled reign, a papal secretary named Flavio Biondo began to catalogue the ruins of ancient Rome systematically, measuring the broken buildings and digging up old streets. The Florentine artists Brunelleschi and Donatello had pioneered this work in the early part of the century, but their interest was primarily architectural and artistic. Biondo had a more political vision; in searching through the ruins he hoped to reconstruct the glory of ancient Rome and bring it into the present under the rule of the papacy. Biondo published the results of his architectural work in three volumes entitled *Rome Restored* (1444–46) and later outlined his political vision in *Rome Triumphant* (1459).

The rebirth of Rome as a Renaissance city began with Nicholas V, who reigned from 1447 to 1455, the first pope in 150 years to spend his entire reign in Rome. Born the son of a poor Tuscan physician, Nicholas became a close friend of Cosimo de' Medici, who commissioned him to catalogue the great library of Niccolò Niccoli. He avidly read the new learning discovered by the Florentine humanists and watched artists like Brunelleschi and Donatello at work. Although many churchmen condemned the new art and learning as "pagan," Nicholas recognized the greatness of Greek and Roman culture.

When he became pope, Nicholas invited artists and humanist scholars to Rome, commissioning works of art and translations of the classics, and collecting books that formed the foundation of the Vatican Library. He began to beautify the city, repairing old churches, bridges, and walls and reconstructing the Roman Capitol; yet he also destroyed pagan temples. He decided to rebuild the crumbling, 1,100-year-old church of St. Peter's into a great domed basilica that would represent Rome the way the domed cathedral represented Florence. Although the walls rose only six feet during Nicholas's time, it was a step in creating a new and beautiful city that would once again become the center of the Christian world. Toward the end of his life, Nicholas also played a key role in Italian politics, leading the way with his old friend Cosimo de' Medici in forging the Peace of Lodi.

As he lay dying, Nicholas explained the reasoning behind his building efforts. To keep their faith strong, he said, ordinary human beings "must have something that appeals to the eye . . . majestic buildings, imperishable memorials and witnesses seemingly planted by the hand of God."

In 1458, three years after Nicholas's death, another Tuscan humanist, Aeneas Silvius, became Pope Pius II, one of the most learned men ever to sit on the throne of St. Peter. By the time he entered the priesthood in his early forties, he had established himself among the leading writers and diplomats of the age, traveling throughout Europe, serving cardinals, the antipope Felix, and the Holy Roman Emperor—

who honored him as poet laureate. After becoming pope, he wrote an autobiography called *Commentaries* that provides fascinating insight into the times. Pius was a brilliant egotist who had a low opinion of many Renaissance leaders, but he saved his most scathing criticism for the corruption within the Church:

> Like businessmen who have failed to pay their creditors, we have no credit left. The priesthood is an object of scorn. They say we live for pleasure, hoard up money, serve ambition, sit on mules or pedigree horses, spread out the fringes of our cloaks and go about the city with fat cheeks under our red hats and ample hoods, that we breed dogs for hunting, spend freely upon players and parasites, but nothing in defense of the Faith. Nor is it all a lie!

Although disgusted by the corruption he saw around him, Pius made three members of his own family cardinals and gave his sisters lavish palaces and incomes. Nonetheless, his rule continued the strengthening of the papacy and the development of Rome as a Renaissance city. As a biographer pointed out, Pius himself was one of the most representative figures of the Renaissance: "A shrewd statesman, an elegant humanist, an inquiring traveler—keenly addicted to the learning of the past, but equally alive to any new ideas or discoveries of his own time—witty and urbane, skeptical and adaptable . . ." Yet, at the height of his career, he embarked on the last Crusade to defeat the "infidel" Turks, a hopeless cause more in keeping with the ideals of the Middle Ages. He aroused little support for the project and died in the Italian coastal city of Ancona, while waiting for ships to take him and his armies to the east.

Pius and Nicholas were unusual among the popes in that they were born into poor families and rose to high position through their own brilliance and scholarship. Paul II, who followed Pius in 1464, was born into a wealthy Venetian family and his uncle, Pope Eugenius IV, made him a cardinal at the age of 25. He amassed the finest collection of ancient coins and artifacts of the time; but despite his interest in the objects of the past, he dismissed the humanist scholars who had begun to dominate the papal bureaucracy under Nicholas and Pius. When the humanists protested, Paul retaliated by proclaiming that much of the "pagan" learning should be outlawed. This was a temporary setback for Renaissance culture in Rome, but Paul also added to the prestige and beauty of the city. He encouraged celebrations, offered increased indulgences to religious pilgrims, and continued the restoration and building programs of his predecessors.

Paul II was a transitional figure in the development of the Renaissance papacy, a bridge between the scholarly humanists before him and the men who followed: ruthless, worldly leaders who viewed the papacy as a source of wealth and secular power rather than a high religious office. And yet it was these violent, often lusty men—more princes than popes—who raised Rome above other Italian cities and ushered in the highest level of Renaissance art and culture.

THE POLITICAL POPES AND THE HIGH RENAISSANCE

Sixtus IV, who reigned from 1471 to 1484, took the practice of nepotism to new heights—appointing countless relatives to high positions, including his four nephews, one of whom later became Pope Julius II. (Our word *nepotism* comes from the Italian word for nephew.) In the still chaotic and hostile atmosphere of the Papal States, giving power to his family ensured a degree of loyalty and control, as his younger relatives carved out their own territories under his central authority. However, as Sixtus increased his domination of the outlying regions, he was drawn into two wars with other Italian powers.

The first was the war with Florence that followed the Pazzi Conspiracy in 1478, when Sixtus joined with the Florentine Pazzi family in an attempt to assassinate Lorenzo de' Medici and take control of Florence. It's typical of Renaissance politics in general—and papal politics in particular—that Sixtus called on Naples to fight the war against Florence, but then turned against the papal ally a few years later and sided with Venice in a war against Naples, only to break off with Venice before the war was over! These wars gained nothing, but they established that the Papal States were now a major force among the Italian powers.

Along with his political maneuverings, Sixtus made enormous contributions to the culture of Rome, bringing the humanists back from their temporary exile and adding substantially to the library founded by Nicholas. He widened streets, built bridges and hospitals, and

While Renaissance popes concentrated on worldly matters, fiery "preachers of repentance" drew large crowds by denouncing the corruption of the Church and demanding that people mend their ways. This panel painting by Bartolomeo Degli Erri (c. 1485) portrays St. Vincent Ferrer preaching outside a church in Verona. (Ashmolean Museum, Oxford)

encouraged construction throughout the city. His greatest monument was the Sistine Chapel, named after himself and decorated by the finest artists of the time. He established the Sistine choir, which gave Rome a reputation for excellence in music, and he threw banquets and entertainments on a level that had not been seen since the days of the Roman emperors.

The pope who followed Sixtus, Innocent VIII (1484–92), was a weak ruler, who spent most of his time and money financing the exploits of his illegitimate children and grandchildren. (By the time

LUCREZIA BORGIA: THE WOMAN BEHIND THE REPUTATION

The name Lucrezia Borgia has come down in history as a symbol of murder, incest, and other immoral behavior. As is often the case with such historical reputations, it's based more on rumor than reality. However, Lucrezia's real story reveals much about Renaissance politics and the role of women in the powerful, wealthy families of the time.

Born in 1480 to Cardinal Rodrigo Borgia and his mistress, Vanozza Catanei, Lucrezia was educated in a convent and enjoyed a pleasant childhood. However, her childhood ended abruptly at the age of 12, when her father became Pope Alexander VI, and she became a pawn in his political ambitions. Hoping to strengthen his ties with Milan, Alexander arranged for Lucrezia to be married to Giovanni Sforza, nephew of the Milanese ruler Lodovico Sforza. The marriage proved unhappy and childless, and five years later Alexander had it annulled—the only form of legal separation allowed by the Church.

According to Church law at the time, a marriage could be annulled only if the husband was unable to consummate it by having sexual relations with his wife. Giovanni fought the annulment and accused Alexander of having incestuous relations with Lucrezia. Although Alexander loved his daughter deeply, there is no evidence to support this claim, but it was the beginning of a series of ugly rumors about Lucrezia, her father, and her brothers, that created much of the dark legend connected with her name.

After the marriage was annulled in December 1497, Alexander arranged a new marriage—with Don Alfonso, the illegitimate son of the heir to the throne of Naples. Ironically, Lucrezia's first marriage had been an attempt by Alexander to strengthen his hand *against* Naples, but now he saw his daughter as a way to improve his relations with the power to the south. This time, Lucrezia—now a "mature" woman of 18—fell in love

with her 17-year-old husband and gave birth to a son. Shortly after the marriage, Alexander appointed Lucrezia regent of Spoleto—an unusual political post for a woman of the time, in which Lucrezia served with distinction.

Unfortunately, a bitter conflict developed between Lucrezia's husband and her brother Cesare, and Alfonso was stabbed while leaving St. Peter's Church in July 1500. Although he recovered from his wounds, Alfonso assumed that the assassins were sent by Cesare, and he attacked his wife's brother with a bow and arrow, narrowly missing. Cesare retaliated by having his guards suffocate Alfonso with a pillow. It's possible that Lucrezia was forced to watch the murder, but she certainly had no part in it. Yet again, Rome buzzed with ugly rumors about the daughter of the pope.

Although her beloved Alfonso's death plunged Lucrezia into misery, she remained loyal to her brother, apparently believing that his actions were justified by Alfonso's attack with the bow and arrow. A year later, Alexander arranged yet another political marriage, this time to Alfonso d'Este, son of the Duke of Ferrara. The Este were an old ruling family, and though Alexander promised a huge dowry, they were concerned by Lucrezia's reputation. So they asked their ambassador in Rome to meet her and report on her character. He gave her nothing but praise:

> She is a most intelligent and lovely, and also an exceedingly gracious, lady. . . . Besides being extremely graceful in every way, she is modest, lovable, and decorous. Moreover, she is a devout and God-fearing Christian. . . . She is very beautiful, but her charm of manner is still more striking. In short, her character is such that it is impossible to suspect anything "sinister" of her; but on the contrary we look for only the best . . .

The Este accepted the marriage, and Pope Alexander sent his beloved daughter off to Ferrara with a huge procession that included 180 people and 150 mules. Her wedding dress alone was valued at 15,000 ducats, at a time when one ducat would purchase a small book. When Lucrezia arrived in Ferrara, all the prisoners were released in her honor and the

people rejoiced in their future duchess.

Although their marriage was strictly political, Lucrezia had seven children with Alfonso d'Este, four of whom lived to adulthood. As duchess of Ferrara she presided over a glittering court and became an important patron of the arts. She wrote poetry in several languages, and exchanged passionate letters with several courtiers, including the courtly poet Pietro Bembo. Some earlier historians assumed that Lucrezia and Bembo were lovers—which added to her reputation for immorality—but it is more likely that their letters reflected the Renaissance ideal of perfect platonic (nonsexual) love.

She had come to them with a questionable reputation, but the people of Ferrara loved and appreciated Lucrezia for her goodness and generosity. Like many women of her time, Lucrezia Borgia died in childbirth. She was only 39 years old, but it seemed that she had already lived several lives.

of the Renaissance, the clergy were not allowed to marry, but mistresses and illegitimate children were common, especially among the wealthy bishops and cardinals of the Church.) During his reign, Roman control of the Papal States fell into decline, but the next pope reversed the trend with a vengeance.

Rodrigo Borgia became Pope Alexander VI in 1492 in what has been called the most corrupt election in papal history, and he ultimately aroused more negative feeling among the Italians than any other pope of the time. Although corruption was not unusual in papal elections, much of the Italian outrage stemmed from the Spanish origins of the Borgia family, who originally came to Rome with Rodrigo's uncle, Pope Calixtus III (1455–58). However, it's true that Alexander was a strong-willed, sensual man who had four children by one mistress before becoming pope and at least two children by other mistresses after ascending the throne of St. Peter.

Alexander's reputation for ruthless cruelty is really based on the actions of his son, Cesare, who was much admired by the famous political writer Niccolò Machiavelli. Educated in the new learning,

Cesare had risen to the rank of cardinal as his father's closest advisor. But after the mysterious death of his older brother in 1498—which some blamed on Cesare—he renounced his Church offices and began a military campaign to force the rebellious cities of the Papal States into submission. Cesare was a man of great physical strength and personal charm who could draw his enemies toward him with soothing words and then have them executed in the blink of an eye. The tactic was eminently successful, and by 1502 he had subdued or killed most of the rebellious signori and barons of the papal cities. However, his father's death the following year ended his base of power, and Cesare was forced to flee from Rome during the reign of Julius II.

Julius (1503–1513) was a warrior himself and a staunch enemy of the Borgia family, although he used Cesare to put down a rebellion before stripping him of his power. Sixty years old when he ascended to the papacy, Julius had the powerful build and constitution of a much younger man, and he liked nothing more than to ride on a fine warhorse in a good suit of armor. In 1506 he became the first pope ever to ride out of Rome at the head of an army, as he began a highly successful campaign to subdue the rebellious Papal States once and for all. Julius also led his armies against Venice, which was expanding into papal territory, and against the French, winning a key battle over the city of Mirandola that proved a turning point in the French expulsion from Italy in 1513.

Despite his warlike nature, Julius was one of the greatest papal patrons of art, and it was during his reign that Rome exploded with the full glory of the High Renaissance. Julius commissioned Michelangelo to paint the ceiling of the Sistine Chapel, perhaps the most exquisite single achievement of Renaissance art. He commissioned Raphael to paint pictures in a series of Vatican rooms called the *Stanze*, ordering the artist to plaster over the work of older masters and begin anew with the highly developed eye of the early 16th century. Finally, Julius commissioned the architect Donato Bramante to begin work on the basilica of St. Peter's, the grand project envisioned by Nicholas V some 60 years earlier.

When Julius died in 1513, he was succeeded by the 37-year-old Giovanni de' Medici, second son of Lorenzo the Magnificent, who took the name Leo X. His father had groomed him for the papacy from an early age, and through Lorenzo's influence, Giovanni took minor Church orders at the age of eight, became an abbot at 12, and was a cardinal at 13! By the time he was elected pope, there was a such an inevitability about the idea that Leo supposedly said, "Let us enjoy the papacy since God has given it to us."

Enjoy it he did. With his family background of enormous wealth, Leo loved extravagant celebrations, and he marked the beginning of his reign with a gala procession through the streets of Rome. This reflected Leo's own tastes, but it also indicated the stronger state of the papacy. Less than a century earlier, in the days of Martin and Eugenius, no pope would have dared such a public display. Now all Rome welcomed him, and for the day at least, the squabbling cardinals and nobles forgot their differences.

Leo continued Julius's lavish patronage of art and learning. Although he enjoyed comedies in Italian, he had a special love of the Latin language and invited almost 300 Latin poets to Rome, where they lived at the pope's expense. He commissioned Raphael to create a set of tapestries for the Sistine Chapel and hired him to continue work on St. Peter's after Bramante's death. He hunted in the Roman countryside and gave generous gifts to the peasants who lined the road to greet him. All of this cost money, and Leo paid for it by selling Church offices and indulgences on a greater scale than ever before—a practice that provoked the religious reformer Martin Luther to attack the Catholic Church in 1517. Although Leo excommunicated Luther in 1521, the full impact of the Protestant Reformation did not emerge until later, and Leo ruled in a period of relative calm between the foreign invasions that shook Italy during the late 15th and early 16th centuries. As historian John R. Hale points out, "In retrospect it was not unsuitable to describe [Leo's] pontificate—like his father's period of control in Florence—as a Golden Age."

Six years after Leo's death, another Medici sat on the papal throne. But Clement VII was not as fortunate as his cousin and predecessor had been. In May 1527, the troops of Holy Roman Emperor Charles V sacked the city of Rome, imprisoned Clement, and drove him into exile. Although he later returned—and Rome continued to be an important cultural center—the great age of the Roman Renaissance was over. Now Venice became the golden city.

p. 36   "must have something . . ." Nicholas V; quoted in Vincent Cronin. *The Flowering of the Renaissance* (New York: E. P. Dutton, 1969), p. 25.

p. 37   "Like businessmen . . ." Pius II, *Commentaries;* quoted in Iris Origo. "Pope Pius II," in *Horizon Book,* p. 227.

p. 37   "A shrewd statesman . . ." Origo. p. 227.

p. 41   "She is a most intelligent . . ." Joannes Lucas; quoted in Will Durant. *The Renaissance,* The Story of Civilization, vol. 5 (New York: Simon & Schuster, 1953), p. 432.

p. 44   "Let us enjoy . . ." Leo X; quoted in John R. Hale, ed. *A Concise Encyclopedia of the Renaissance,* (New York: Oxford University Press, 1981), p. 182.

p. 44   "In retrospect . . ." John R. Hale. p. 183.

VENICE, MILAN, AND NAPLES:

Powers of North and South

Although Florence and Rome are the two cities most closely associated with the art and learning of the Italian Renaissance, the other great powers, Venice, Milan, and Naples, played important roles in the politics of the time, and to a somewhat lesser extent, in the arts. Then, in the mid-16th century, as Renaissance culture faded elsewhere in Italy, Venice took center stage as the city of artists and celebration.

VENICE: CITY OF SPLENDOR

Separated from the Italian mainland by its lagoons, Venice developed separately from the other city-states. The city's wealth depended on trade with the eastern Mediterranean, and during the early Renaissance, the Venetians were more concerned with events in the Byzantine Empire than with events in Italy. In 1380 Venice defeated Genoa for supremacy of the sea and established a series of trading bases along the eastern coast of the Adriatic and in the eastern Mediterranean, making Venice the only power in Europe with an overseas empire— until the later colonization of Africa and the New World.

The tool of Venice's trade was its fleet of swift ships called galleys, built under government supervision in the state-owned arsenal. Venetian galleys brought luxuries from the East: spices, silks, slaves, carpets, gold, silver, and jewels. From western Europe, galleys and overland traders brought simpler goods: wood, furs, wool, cloth, wine, copper, and iron. Venice served as a middleman between East and West, and this trade made the Venetian people very rich.

At least some of the Venetian people were rich. Venice was the only Italian city-state to remain a constitutional republic throughout the Renaissance, but it was a strange sort of republic. As in Florence, power rested in the hands of wealthy merchants, but Venice did not share the Florentine tradition of popular participation. Citizenship was limited to the men of about 200 families, and the offspring of these families was carefully catalogued in the *Libro d'Oro,* the Golden Book. The ceremonial head of state, called the *doge,* served for life, but real power rested in the Senate and the Council of Ten, which controlled state security. Although Venice had a glittering gaiety on the surface, the Council of Ten ruthlessly disposed of anyone who threatened the Venetian economy.

Despite this ruthlessness in economic matters, Venice was an extremely tolerant, cosmopolitan city on a social level. In Venetian wharves and warehouses, Greeks, Jews, Turks, and Armenians mingled with Germans, Dutch, French, and English. This mixture of Christians and "infidels" shocked many Europeans, but it made for a fascinating, colorful city.

Venice became more involved in Italian affairs in the early 15th century, when it began to expand inland through a series of expensive wars fought by mercenary armies. This was a sharp departure for the city, which had always looked out toward the sea. But the Venetians wanted to secure their trading routes over the Alps into western Europe while also gaining control over nearby farmlands to ensure a steady food supply. Among its first conquests were the cities of Verona and Padua, the heart of early Renaissance humanism. Soon the sons of

Venice in a woodcut depicting activity along the Grand Canal, with the mainland of Italy in the background. (From Mainz, *Sanctarum Peregrinationum Opusculum,* 1486; USZ62-41780, Rosenwald Collection, Rare Book Division, Library of Congress)

wealthy Venetian families were studying at the University of Padua and returning home to spread the new learning.

As Venice became interested in Renaissance ideas, the city's location and role in trade made it a leading center for the development of ideas from other countries. While the humanists of Florence and Rome were skeptical of the new German invention called the printing press, Venice became the most important printing center in Europe, publishing one fourth of the world's books by the end of the 15th century. At the same time, Venice's close relationship with the eastern Mediterranean made it a natural center for Greek scholars who fled the Byzantine Empire after the fall of Constantinople in 1453. Venetian artists learned the techniques of oil painting from the artists of Flanders—an old Venetian trading partner—and began to develop a unique style of painting that used oils to create a lustrous sense of light.

Venetian expansion and prosperity aroused the envy of other powers, both in Italy and in the rest of Europe. Beginning in December 1508, France, Spain, the Holy Roman Empire, the papacy, and the smaller Italian city-states of Mantua and Ferrara all joined together in the League of Cambrai and agreed to attack Venice and divide the spoils. On May 14, 1509, the French army handed Venice a resounding

THE ITALIAN RENAISSANCE

defeat at Agnadello, and the Venetians lost the majority of their inland possessions. But the league began to collapse the following year, and by 1517, Venice had regained most of its lost territory.

After the sack of Rome in 1527 by the Holy Roman Empire, Venice carried on the gay pageantry and artistic life of the Renaissance. But it was a different sort of culture from the culture celebrated in Florence and Rome. While the Florentine Renaissance had youthful vigor and the Roman Renaissance unparalleled brilliance, the Venetian Renaissance had an older feeling of elegance and splendor.

With their enormous wealth, the Venetians built marble palaces in the city and exquisite villas in the countryside, where they escaped from the summer heat and danced the night away. They decorated their walls with paintings of themselves, and Venetian artists—including the great Titian—developed portrait painting to a high art. For their wealthy patrons, Venetian craftsmen turned out luxury goods that permeated the life of the city: bronze statues that looked like antiques, exquisite glassware, dazzling jewelry, and delicate lace. There were elegant books, too, although Venice's greatest printer, Aldus Manutius, turned out simpler, well-made volumes that filled the library of every learned Venetian—and libraries throughout Europe.

While the rest of Italy fell under foreign domination, Venice maintained its independence and its mainland territories long after the Renaissance was over, finally falling to Napoleon Bonaparte in 1797. However, during the 16th century—even as its citizens celebrated the good life of the late Renaissance—Venice's wealth and power faded when European trade turned toward the New World across the Atlantic and away from the ancient world of the eastern Mediterranean. By 1585, the once-mighty Venetian economy had collapsed, with 96 out of 103 banks in bankruptcy.

In 1495, just as Venice began to enter its own golden age as a Renaissance city, a French ambassador described it with awe and wonder:

> . . . the houses are very large and lofty, and built of stone; the old ones are all painted, those of about a hundred years standing are faced with white marble from Istria . . . and inlaid with porphyry and serpentine. Within they have . . . rich marble chimney-

pieces, bedsteads of gold color, their portals of the same, and most gloriously furnished. In short, it is the most triumphant city that I have ever seen, the most respectful to all ambassadors and strangers, governed with the greatest wisdom, and serving God with the most solemnity.

A century later, the stone buildings still stood, and the Venetian people still treated strangers well and worshipped God solemnly. But the city was no longer triumphant, for the world had passed it by. The Renaissance had passed as well—in Venice and in Italy.

MILAN: CITY OF TYRANTS

Milan—under the shadow of the Alps on the fertile plain of Lombardy—was the most aggressive and despotic of the Italian city-states. In the late 13th century, the noble Visconti family took control and gradually turned the city into an absolute, hereditary *signoria* (the domain of a *signore* or a political strongman). Although they taxed the people heavily and ruled with an iron hand, the Visconti provided strong leadership that made Milan one of the wealthiest and most powerful forces in Italy.

The rule of the Visconti reached its climax with Gian Galeazzo, who inherited some territories on the death of his father in 1378 and grabbed the rest by murdering his uncle in 1385. A man of intelligence and overwhelming ambition, Gian Galeazzo was accepted among the highest nobility of Europe. At the age of nine, he had been married to a French princess, and he later arranged a marriage between his daughter and the French royal family—establishing a "French Connection" that would ultimately prove fatal to the Italian Renaissance. Visconti further strengthened his family's noble credentials by buying the title duke of Milan from the Holy Roman Emperor in 1395.

Gian Galeazzo ruled Milan more judiciously than most Visconti. He reduced taxes, brought humanists to his court, collected manuscripts, and supported the University of Pavia. However, it was as a diplomat and military leader that he left his strongest mark. Under his leadership, Milan conquered much of northern Italy, and it was only his early death in 1402 that stopped the Milanese army from overrunning Florence. Although his propagandists claimed that Gian Galeazzo was waging a noble campaign to unify the Italian peninsula, many historians question such a grand vision. After his death, his "empire" quickly collapsed.

Gian Galeazzo's older son, Giovanni Maria, ruled for 10 years with such insane tyranny that his assassination in church caused little surprise—and much relief among the people. He was succeeded as duke of Milan by his younger brother Filippo Maria, who began to put his father's territories back together. But though he brought the nearby cities and countryside under Milanese control, he met fierce resistance from a united Venice and Florence when he tried to expand further.

Unlike his father, Filippo Maria was a timid soul who depended completely on condottieri (mercenary soldier-captains) to fight his wars. One of these condottieri, Francesco Sforza, grew so powerful that Filippo Maria offered him the hand of his daughter in marriage. When Filippo Maria died in 1447 without a male heir, Milan experimented briefly with a republic. But three years later, with the republic a hopeless failure, Sforza was granted the title of duke by the citizens and a new dynasty was born.

Francesco Sforza was a strong-willed yet reasonable man, and for the most part the people of Milan welcomed his rule after the long, tyrannical reign of the Visconti. Sforza was further supported by one of the most important men of the time, Cosimo de' Medici of Florence. Disturbed by Venetian expansion, Cosimo saw friendship with Sforza as a way to maintain the balance of power in the north and keep the mountain passes open for Florentine traders. This was a shift in policy for Florence, which had been a traditional enemy of Milan, but it led to the Peace of Lodi in 1454, in which the major powers accepted their borders and recognized the Sforza dynasty.

When Francesco died in 1466, his son Galeazzo Maria became duke of Milan. In a strange echo of the Visconti dynasty, Galeazzo embarked on a 10-year rule of such tyranny and greed that he was assassinated in church. Upon Galeazzo's death, the hereditary dukedom passed to his seven-year-old son, Gian Galeazzo II, with the boy's mother ruling as regent. In the chaotic politics of Renaissance Italy, and especially in the murderous world of Milan, this situation opened up far too many possibilities for intrigue. In 1480 the young duke's uncle, Lodovico il Moro, imprisoned the boy's mother and took over the state as regent, while allowing his nephew to continue as the "puppet-duke."

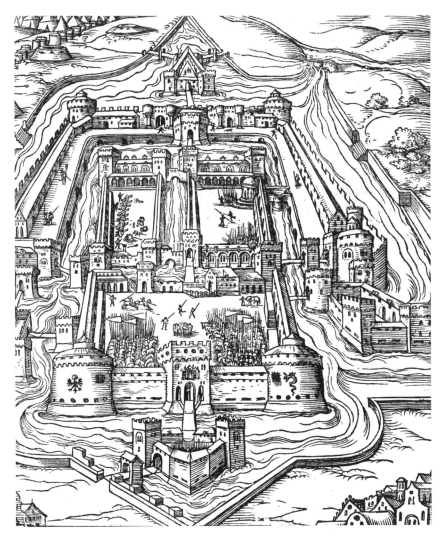

The Sforza Castle in Milan was built by Francesco Sforza as an impenetrable fortress, but his sons Gian Galeazzo and Lodovico used it for some of the most lavish spectacles of the Renaissance. (From Sebastian Muenster, *Cosmographia*, 1588; Rare Books Division, Library of Congress)

The rule of Lodovico was the high point of the Renaissance in Milan. He married the beautiful, cultured Beatrice d'Este, and staged celebrations that matched the gaudiest festivals of Florence, Venice, and Rome. He hired the architect Donato Bramante to supervise an ambitious building program, had canals dug to irrigate the countryside, and encouraged rice and other new crops among the farmers of the Lombard plain. He supported Leonardo da Vinci for almost 20 years, though his patronage was based more on Leonardo's designs for theatrical entertainments and military fortifications than on his artistic ability. Leonardo filled thousands of pages with notes and sketches during his years in Milan, but completed few paintings, most notably his famous fresco, *The Last Supper*.

When his nephew died in 1494, Lodovico was officially granted the title of duke. Although this should have been his crowning glory, it proved the beginning of the end of the Sforza dynasty—and the Italian Renaissance. Caught up in the extremely complex politics of the time, Lodovico actively supported the invasion of French King Charles VIII, allowing French troops to march freely through Milanese territory on their way to Naples. Lodovico then turned against the French and worked to remove the foreign power. This double-cross proved especially dangerous because the French royal family had claims on Milan that dated to the old connection with the Visconti family. In 1499, when the French invaded again, Lodovico was driven from the city. He returned briefly the following year, but the French captured him and he ultimately died in a dark French prison cell.

NAPLES: KINGDOM OF THE SOUTH

Of the five great powers, Naples was the most backward economically and politically. Its economy was based almost completely on agriculture, and except for a few regions, the farmland of southern Italy was poor. The political structure never progressed beyond the feudal system of the Middle Ages. A small group of non-Italian nobles lived in outrageous wealth, while lesser nobles fought for what little wealth remained. The vast majority of the people were farmers who lived in terrible poverty, scratching a meager living from the land, while the nobles took most of what they produced. Unlike the north, Naples had no real middle class, and most finance and trade was handled by men from Florence and other Italian cities.

Despite this backward system, Naples produced several periods of cultural achievement and played an extremely important role in the politics of Italy during the Renaissance. This importance did not lie so

---

much in Naples itself, but in its strong connections with other European powers. In the 13th century, the Holy Roman Emperor Frederick II—who made his court on the island of Sicily—also controlled Naples and the countryside of southern Italy. Frederick was a highly intelligent, cultured man who wrote poetry in an early form of Italian, founded the University of Naples, and surrounded himself with writers, philosophers, and scientists. Some historians view Frederick's reign as a sort of pre-Renaissance, but despite his personal genius, Frederick was very much a medieval despot. It is said that, in order to carry out a "scientific" experiment, he fed two of his men a good dinner, sent one to sleep and ordered the other to go hunting. He then had them disemboweled before his eyes to see which man had digested his food better.

Frederick's death in 1250 plunged Naples into confusion, along with most of Italy and the Holy Roman Empire. In 1266, at the invitation of the pope, the French royal family of Anjou took control of Frederick's holdings in southern Italy. In 1282, however, a popular revolt drove the Anjou from Sicily, and they were replaced by the Spanish royal family of Aragon, while the Anjou continued to rule the mainland. This set up a conflict between France and Spain that culminated over two centuries later in the foreign invasions that ended the Italian Renaissance.

The rule of Robert of Anjou from 1309 to 1343 brought early Renaissance culture to Naples. Robert patronized the great artists and writers of the time, including Giotto, Petrarch, and Boccaccio. He also played an important role in defending Italy from the invasions of the Holy Roman Emperors. In return for his efforts, he was awarded control over five towns in Tuscany and a province in the Papal States, along with his kingdom in the south. Perhaps the most important political figure of his time, his admirers called him "Robert the Wise." On the other hand, the poet Dante, who supported the emperor, scornfully labeled him "the preacher king."

Robert's death, followed five years later by the Black Death, began another period of political chaos and economic hardship. Naples was hit especially hard by the plague, because its economy depended on large numbers of agricultural workers rather than on trade or finance. One third of the villages in southern Italy were abandoned as their people died. In the meantime, Robert's heirs squabbled over control of the kingdom. He was succeeded by his granddaughter, Giovanna I, who murdered three husbands and ended up being murdered herself in 1382. The kingdom then passed to another branch of the Anjou family, who fought among themselves and with the Aragons of Sicily well into the 15th century.

The situation finally stabilized in February 1443, when Alfonso of Aragon marched into the city of Naples as ruler of the Kingdom of Naples, which reunited Sicily and the southern mainland. Alfonso brought a new period of culture to Naples, earning the title "Alfonso the Magnanimous" for his lavish patronage of arts and learning. He attracted leading humanist scholars to his court and beautified the city with a building program similar to those undertaken by the popes and rulers of the north. He contributed greatly to the University of Naples and founded a new university and a school for Greek studies on Sicily. Although Alfonso taxed the people heavily to pay for this cultural Renaissance, he provided a measure of peace and stability that made them look back on his reign as a golden age.

When Alfonso died in 1458, he divided his kingdom, leaving Sicily to his brother Giovanni while giving Naples to his illegitimate son Ferrante. In effect, this marked the end of the Renaissance in Naples. The stability that Alfonso had created unraveled quickly under Ferrante, as he faced an attempted invasion by the Anjou family, a peasant revolt, and a rebellion of his feudal barons. Ferrante did not possess his father's "magnanimous" nature, and he fought these insurrections with ruthless cruelty. When Ferrante died in 1494, Charles VIII of France was already preparing his invasion of Italy, with the intention of throwing the Aragon family out and replacing them with his own French rule. Thus, the Kingdom of Naples, which played a relatively small part in Renaissance culture, actually sparked the foreign invasions that ended the Italian Renaissance.

CHAPTER 5 NOTE

p. 49   ". . . the houses are very large . . ." Philippe de Commines; quoted in Hale. p. 34.

THE SMALLER CITY-STATES:

Democrats and Dukes

Five great powers dominated Italy during the 15th century. However, in the early years of the Renaissance, other cities played key roles in culture, politics, and trade. And even after the five powers divided most of the peninsula among them, a few smaller city-states maintained their independence under strong, benevolent princes and flourished with their own Renaissance life. Although we cannot examine each of these cities in depth, a brief survey of the smaller city-states offers a glimpse into the variety of Italy during the Renaissance.

REPUBLICS OF THE EARLY RENAISSANCE

Located on the western coast of the Italian peninsula, Genoa and Pisa emerged as sea powers during the Middle Ages, along with Venice on the eastern coast. In 1284 the Genoese navy defeated Pisa, effectively ending Pisa's power and making Genoa the undisputed master of the western Tyrrhenian Sea. However, the economic opportunities lay in the eastern Mediterranean, where Genoa established a string of trading bases in competition with Venice. In 1380 the Venetian fleet handed Genoa a stinging defeat and Venice took over Genoa's overseas empire.

Despite this setback, Genoa remained a large, thriving city throughout the Renaissance as a center for banking and silk production. However, it exhibited little Renaissance culture. To some extent this was due to the instability of the Genoese republic, which was violently torn by class warfare. In 1339 the city established a doge system, similar to that of Venice, but the Genoese doges rarely lasted—several were driven from power in a single day. Faced with this political chaos, Genoa fell easy prey to foreign powers, including France and Milan. The Genoese admiral, Andrea Doria, finally brought stability in 1528 and introduced the culture of the High Renaissance. A generation earlier, another Genoese seaman named Christopher Columbus had opened up the New World.

Although Pisa never regained its status as a major power after its defeat by Genoa, it continued to control a busy port called Porto Pisano, which aroused the interest of Florence, located up the Arno River. In 1406 Pisa fell to Florence's mercenary armies, and 15 years later Florence bought Porto Pisano from Genoa. Florence was already a wealthy trading center, but the Pisan port allowed Florentine merchants to send their own galleys out to sea rather than depending on Venice or Genoa. Because of its economic importance, many Florentines moved to Pisa, and in 1472, Lorenzo de' Medici revived its university, transferring some of the best faculty from Florence.

While Genoa and Pisa represent the economic power of the early Renaissance, the intellectual revival began in three inland cities of northern Italy: Bologna, Padua, and Verona. It was at the University of Bologna in the 12th century that scholars began to study Roman law with new intensity, uncovering classical manuscripts that ultimately led to the birth of humanism. Although the university continued to be a leading center for legal studies throughout the Renaissance, the city itself was torn by internal conflict, and its local problems were made worse by the chaotic situation in the Papal States—to which it owed nominal allegiance. The Bentivoglio family brought some stability during the latter 15th century, ruling as "first citizens" in a manner similar to the Medici in Florence, but they never achieved the splendor

The women of Siena were famous for their beauty; this young lady was the grandniece of Pope Pius II, who brought a period of relative calm to his native city by controlling its competing factions from Rome. (Neroccio de' Landi, *Portrait of a Lady*, Widener Collection, ©1994 National Gallery of Art, Washington)

THE ITALIAN RENAISSANCE

of their neighbors to the south. In the early 16th century, Bologna was placed firmly under papal rule by Pope Julius II.

Padua and Verona were the cradles of early humanism, where lawyers and notaries began to read Roman poetry and other literature for pleasure and inspiration rather than for an understanding of the law. By 1300, the University of Padua rivaled the University of Bologna, drawing students from all over Europe. But like Bologna, both Padua and Verona were torn by internal conflicts, rooted in the battle between Guelphs and Ghibellines. (The tragic struggle between two leading families of Verona was immortalized in Shakespeare's *Romeo and Juliet*.)They fell under the despotic rule of *signori* during the 14th century, and both were conquered by Venice in 1405. Under Venetian rule, the University of Padua continued as a major cultural force, becoming the most important center for Greek studies and scientific experimentation in the late Renaissance.

Along with Florence and Pisa, Siena and Lucca were the other republics of Tuscany. Although both preserved their independence through much of the Renaissance period, Siena made the most significant cultural contributions. During the early 14th century, while Giotto laid the foundations of Florentine art, the painters of Siena established their own style. But Sienese art never developed as fully as the art of their larger neighbor. As with so many republics, the city's resources were stretched thin by political conflict and warfare. Siena struggled constantly—and unsuccessfully—to find a democratic system that worked, while also resisting a series of attacks by Florence. The long tradition of Sienese democracy finally collapsed in 1487, when an exiled aristocrat named Pandolfo Petrucci seized control of the city government and ruled in the ruthless style of earlier signori in other Italian cities. The Petrucci family dominated Sienese politics until 1524.

BRILLIANT COURTS AND BLOODY BATTLEGROUNDS

Amid the constant conflict of Renaissance Italy, Mantua and Ferrara stand out as the most stable of Italian city-states. Each maintained its independence throughout the Renaissance; each was ruled for 300 years by a single family: the Gonzaga in Mantua, the Este in Ferrara. To a great extent, this stability was a function of location. Spread on the

ISABELLA D'ESTE: THE PRIMA DONNA OF THE WORLD

Born in 1474, Isabella d'Este was the oldest child of the duke and duchess of Ferrara. Like Mantua, Ferrara boasted a famous humanist school, and Isabella and her younger sister Beatrice were educated in the classics along with the boys. Although Beatrice became a cultured woman, Isabella was clearly the star pupil of the family. She mastered Latin and Greek grammar and could effortlessly translate Virgil or Cicero into Italian. She performed songs on the lute, danced beautifully, and embroidered to perfection. Driven by a proud and independent spirit, she eagerly discussed literature with great writers and questions of state with ambassadors and princes.

Before her 16th birthday, Isabella married Francesco Gonzaga, the young marquis of Mantua, and was immediately thrust into the limelight of an important, though small, city-state. With her husband often away on military campaigns, Isabella virtually ruled Mantua and showed an extraordinary talent for diplomacy in the ever-shifting world of Italian politics. Perhaps her finest hour came in 1509, when Francesco was captured by the Venetians. Isabella soothed the fears of her people by ordering her troops on the Venice border to defend their fortresses even if the Venetians paraded Francesco outside the gates and murdered him right before their eyes.

Although her bold approach lifted the spirits of her citizens, Francesco was less than pleased. Upon his release, he wrote her a scathing rebuke: "We are ashamed that it is our fate to have as wife a woman who is always ruled by her head."

Isabella replied with cold confidence: "Your Excellency is

fertile plain of Lombardy along the Po River, Mantua formed a buffer between Milan and Venice, while its neighbor Ferrara formed a buffer between Venice and the Papal States. Although smaller than the major indebted to me as never husband was to wife; nor must Your Excellency think that, even did you love and honor me more than any person in the world, you could repay my good faith."

From this point on, Isabella and Francesco became more distant, and Isabella lost some of her power in Mantua. But she continued to be a generous and opinionated patroness of the arts, filling her elegant study with beautiful books and works of art, all under an ornate ceiling carved with her personal motto, "Neither hope nor fear." She corresponded with many of the great leaders and thinkers of the time and surrounded herself with young women whom she educated and molded in her own independent image.

When Francesco died, Isabella regained substantial power through her influence over her son, Federigo—although she had to play a personal diplomatic game with his mistress. Moving back and forth between Mantua and Rome, she observed firsthand the invasion of the imperial troops in 1527, and with clear political judgment, cast her family's lot with Emperor Charles V. Her house in Rome became a safe haven for refugees, and the Emperor later rewarded her son with the title of duke of Mantua.

In her younger years, Isabella had her portrait done by several great artists, including Leonardo da Vinci. Then, at the age of 60, she sat for one last portrait by Titian, the Venetian master who developed portraiture into a high art. When she saw the painting, Isabella was so displeased with her aged appearance that she ordered Titian to begin again, using an earlier portrait to paint her with the face of a young woman. It was a final act of vanity and artistic judgment.

A poetic cousin once called Isabella "La Prima Donna Del Mondo," the first woman of the world. In the world of the Italian Renaissance, the description seemed accurate.

powers, Mantua and Ferrara were too strong and too far away to be easily conquered, and the city of Mantua was surrounded on three sides by swampy lakes. But along with these geographical blessings, we must credit the ruling families for the peace and independence of their states.

The Gonzaga first came to power in 1328, when Luigi Gonzaga I was appointed captain of the people, a position intended to protect the rights of the middle class. Over the following century, they gradually strengthened their hold over the city and further legitimized their rule by buying the royal title of marquis from the Holy Roman Emperor in 1433. As proven military commanders, the Gonzaga gained wealth and assured Mantuan independence by alternately hiring themselves out to lead the armies of Venice and Milan. Throughout their long reign, the family enjoyed substantial support from the people of Mantua. However, it's hard to say whether this was due to their leadership—which was quite enlightened for the times—or due to the iron cage that they hung high above the central plaza as a final prison for those who opposed them.

In 1423 the Gonzaga family invited the humanist teacher Vittorino da Feltre to establish a school for boys, which became the most famous Renaissance institution below the university level. Among da Feltre's pupils was Lodovico Gonzaga, who ruled as marquis of Mantua for 30 years, from 1448 to 1478. With his strong humanist education, Lodovico brought philosophers and poets to his court and collected manuscripts of the classics and the great Italian writers of the 14th century. He hired the brilliant architect Leon Battista Alberti to design buildings, and convinced the innovative artist Andrea Mantegna to leave his native Padua and become the resident painter of the Gonzaga court.

After Lodovico's long, enlightened rule, his son reigned for six short years, followed by his grandson, Francesco, who ruled for 36 years, from 1484 to 1519. Like most Gonzagas, Francesco distinguished himself on the field of battle, becoming the most important Italian military commander during the early years of the foreign invasions. But it was Francesco's wife, Isabella d'Este, who brought the Gonzaga court to its greatest heights. (See box feature.)

Isabella was the daughter of Ercole d'Este, duke of Ferrara, who shared his neighbor's interest in books and learning. The Este were an old, respected noble family who had a special talent for making powerful marriages. Ercole had married Eleanora of Aragon, the daughter of King Ferrante of Naples. Their son, Alfonso, followed his father as duke of Ferrara and married Lucrezia Borgia, daughter of Pope Alexander VI. Isabella's marriage to Francesco Gonzaga cemented the ties between the two independent cities, and Isabella's sister, Beatrice, made the most splendid marriage of all, to Lodovico Sforza, the wealthy and powerful ruler of Milan. (Lodovico had originally asked for Isabella's hand when she was six years old, but she was already promised to Francesco Gonzaga.)

These marriages were an integral part of Renaissance politics, especially for a small state like Ferrara. Geographically, it was less protected than Mantua, and in 1482 Venice invaded from the north—at the invitation of the pope, who wanted Ferrara for one of his nephews. There was little fighting, and within two years, Duke Ercole managed to forge a peace with the support of his powerful allies in Milan, Florence, and Naples. But the threat of Venetian expansion didn't go away, and in 1509 Mantua and Ferrara joined the League of Cambrai—formed by the papacy, Milan, Spain, France, and the Holy Roman Empire—to drive Venice back to its lagoons. Although Venice ended up regaining most of its territory, Ferrara maintained its independence until 1598, while Mantuan independence lasted until 1632.

Of all the leaders of the small city-states, perhaps the greatest was Federigo da Montefeltro, duke of Urbino, a small, isolated mountain town in central Italy. Although technically part of the Papal States, Urbino remained independent during Federigo's reign, from 1444 to 1482. Unlike Mantua and Ferrara, which had fertile farmland and a navigable river for trade, Urbino had little but the tough fighting spirit of its people. Throughout his life, Federigo earned his living and brought wealth to his domain by hiring himself out as a condottiere to the great states, especially Naples and the papacy. But though he may have been the greatest condottiere of his time, it was as a man of learning, compassion, and courtly manners that he is most remembered.

As a boy, Federigo had been a schoolmate of Lodovico Gonzaga at the humanist school of Vittorino da Feltre, who—Federigo recalled—educated him "in all human excellence." With the wealth from his work as a warrior, Federigo attracted artists, writers, and musicians to his small mountain town, and employed at least five different architects and engineers to build a great palace that embodied his own creative ideas of form, space, and decoration. But Federigo's burning passion was beautiful books, and he set out "to create the finest library since ancient times. He spared neither cost nor labor, and when he knew of a fine book, whether in Italy or not, he would send for it." Federigo had no printed books in his library—only elegant, illuminated, hand-written manuscripts bound and embellished with the finest materials.

In an age when most rulers constantly needed to be on guard against assassination, perhaps the greatest testimony to Federigo da Montefeltro's enlightened rule was the love of his people, described by a contemporary writer:

> When he rode out he met none who did not salute him and ask how he did. He went about with few attendants; none of them armed . . . He would often go afoot through his lands, entering now one shop and now another, and asking the workmen what their calling was, and whether they were in need of aught [any-thing]. So kind was he, that they all loved him as children love their parents. The country he ruled was a wondrous sight.

Unfortunately, Federigo da Montefeltro was an exception among Renaissance rulers. His neighbor and enemy, Sigismondo Malatesta of Rimini, was more typical. Although he too was a brilliant and highly cultured condottiere, he was more famous for double-crossing his employers, and for the cruel and immoral behavior that led Pope Pius II to take the unique step of "canonizing" him to hell. (Canonization is the process by which the Church makes a saint, but Sigismondo was definitely not a saint.)

The leaders of the neighboring city of Perugia were even worse. There, two competing families, the Baglioni and the Oddi, waged a war of such terrible ferocity that the streets ran red with blood. In 1491 the Baglioni hung 130 Oddi supporters in the public square, and the Oddi returned the favor by killing four Baglioni leaders in their beds. For a time the Baglioni emerged victorious, but by 1535, most members of the family had either killed each other or been executed in public. Yet amid the bloodshed, art and culture continued to flourish, and it was in Perugia that Raphael learned his craft.

From strife-torn republics to enlightened duchies to bloody battle-grounds, the smaller city-states convey the astonishing range of Italian life during the Renaissance. But perhaps the most astonishing aspect of all is that—at least for a time in most of these cities—the culture of the Renaissance emerged triumphant.

CHAPTER 6 NOTES

p. 60   "We are ashamed . . ." Francesco Gonzaga; quoted in Maria Bellonci, "Beatrice and Isabella d'Este," in *Horizon Book,* p. 366.

pp. 60–1   "Your Excellency is indebted . . ." Isabella d'Este; quoted in Bellonci. p. 336.

p. 64   "to create the finest library . . ." Vespasiano da Bisticci; quoted in Denis Mack Smith, "Federigo da Montefeltro," in *Horizon Book,* p. 326.

p. 64   "When he rode out . . ." da Bisticci; quoted in Smith. p. 323.

THE HUMANISTS:

Free Spirits in a Free World

The humanists were the intellectual engine that drove the Renaissance. They created books by discovering and translating old manuscripts and writing new works based on classical ideals. They served as secretaries and counselors to popes and kings, democrats and tyrants. They educated the children of the great families, producing generations of leaders raised in the humanist tradition. Most important of all, they eloquently expressed the basic philosophy of the times—a philosophy of human potential and realistic observation that led to the beauty of Renaissance art, the beginnings of modern science, and indeed the beginnings of modern life.

The term *humanism* comes from the Latin word *humanitas*, which refers to the complete development of human virtue—including qualities like personal goodness and compassion that we might associate with the word *virtue,* as well as more active qualities like bravery, honor, judgment, and eloquence. The humanists followed a course of classical study, the *studia humanitatis*, that included five major disciplines: grammar, poetry, rhetoric, history, and moral philosophy.

Although many humanists attended or taught at universities, humanism was not an academic movement. Rather it was a point of view and an approach to classical study that passed from man to man, and in a few cases, from man to woman.

The first great humanist was Petrarch, who lived from 1304 to 1374. He called books "gay, useful, and ready-spoken companions," embracing long-dead Roman writers as living forces in his own world—as real or more real than the chaotic Italy outside his study, and far more real than the long, dark age of ignorance that separated him from them. Petrarch searched for the most correct manuscripts, trying to understand the precise meanings of the words the ancients used and to employ their style and vocabulary in his own writing. This concern with pure Latin expression became a key aspect of humanism; at the same time, Petrarch also wrote poetry in the Italian language of Dante, showing a respect for the vernacular that many later humanists resisted.

Petrarch led the way toward a more modern view of humankind by analyzing his own life down to its smallest details. He believed that a poet could be a moral force and a philosophical teacher for his society, and he was crowned poet laureate for his cultural contributions. Yet he was caught between the medieval ideal that a scholar should withdraw from the world and the emerging humanist ideal that a scholar should take an active part in that world. Petrarch's own nature favored the quiet life, but he traveled throughout Italy, entertained and supported by wealthy men of state.

Petrarch's friend, Giovanni Boccaccio, also rediscovered Latin manuscripts and wrote literary and philosophical works in the classical style. But his greatest contribution was his collection of stories, the *Decameron*, written in Italian prose. On one level, the *Decameron* is a collection of 100 stories about love, often bawdy and funny, intended for light reading by cultured ladies. However, these stories also demonstrate a new, realistic way of looking at human nature—not as it should be, but as it is. (For more on Petrarch and Boccaccio, see Chapter 2.)

THE HUMANISTS OF THE EARLY FIFTEENTH CENTURY

The first great circle of humanists arose in Florence around the turn of the 15th century, and the center of the circle was Coluccio Salutati, the chancellor (official secretary) of the city. Born in 1331, Salutati was a much-younger friend of Petrarch, forming a bridge between the early humanism of the 14th century and the full flowering of humanism in the 15th century.

Salutati's official, political writing is discussed in Chapter 3, and he made many contributions to humanist literature. However, more important than his own writing was his discovery of Cicero's *Familiar Letters* in 1392. The philosophy of Cicero had been known throughout the Middle Ages, but medieval scholars imagined him living the solitary, contemplative life that was then considered the ideal. The *Familiar Letters* revealed a financially successful, married man who took an active part in civic affairs and died for his devotion to liberty. It was this new ideal that Salutati conveyed to the people of Florence and to the humanists around him.

As the early humanists examined Latin manuscripts, they realized that much of Roman thought was based on the writing and culture of Greece. There were a few Greek manuscripts available—Petrarch had owned a copy of Homer, which he would kiss reverently; but he couldn't read it, and neither could anyone else in northern Italy. In 1397 Salutati convinced the Florentine leaders to hire Manuel Chrysolorus, a Greek scholar from Constantinople, to teach at the University of Florence. When he departed three years later, Chrysolorus left behind a book on Greek grammar and a nucleus of Florentine humanists who had learned the fundamentals of the Greek language and had developed enormous respect and enthusiasm for the achievements of ancient Greece.

One of Chrysolorus's pupils was Leonardo Bruni, a younger protégé of Salutati who later served as Florentine chancellor himself. With his combined knowledge of Latin and Greek, Bruni became the most important figure in Florentine humanism during the first half of the 15th century. He staunchly defended the ideal of the Florentine Republic and wrote a *History of the Florentine People*, which marked a turning point in the concept of history. Whereas medieval histories were based on legends, hearsay, and signs from God, Bruni used a wide variety of sources and attempted to tell what happened and why it happened based on an actual understanding of people and events.

Bruni also expanded the concept of humanism itself. While Salutati had defined *humanitas* as simply "moral learning," Bruni gave it a

The Byzantine scholar Manuel Chrysolorus, who laid the foundations for Greek studies in Florence. (From Bullart, *Académie des Sciences et des Arts*, Amsterdam, 1682; Rare Book Division, Library of Congress)

deeper meaning, saying that the humanities "are so called, because they bring our humanity to completeness." When the Florentines began to use the term "liberal arts" to refer to the *studia humanitatis*, Bruni eloquently explained: "The liberal arts owe their name to the fact

This fresco by Vincenzo Foppa (c. 1460) was once thought to represent a boy reading Cicero as part of his humanist education; however, art historians now believe it represents Cicero himself studying as a boy, and it has been retitled The Young Cicero Reading. *(Reproduced by permission of the Trustees of the Wallace Collection)*

that they liberate man and make him master of himself in a free world of free spirits."

Another Salutati protégé who later became chancellor of Florence was Poggio Bracciolini, one of the most successful manuscript hunters of the Renaissance. In the summer of 1416, Poggio visited the Irish monastery of St. Gall in what is now Germany. There in the neglected library, "a most foul and dimly lighted dungeon at the very bottom of a tower," he discovered a complete manuscript of *The Training of an Orator* by Quintilian, which set forth a comprehensive Roman educational system. In describing his find, Poggio discussed the dusty manuscript as if it were the man who wrote it:

> I truly believe that, had we not come to the rescue, this man Quintilian must speedily have perished; for it cannot be imagined that a man magnificent, polished, elegant, urbane and witty could much longer have endured the squalor of the prison-house in which I found him. . . . He was indeed a sad sight: ragged, like a

condemned criminal, with rough beard and matted hair, protesting by his expression and dress against the injustice of his sentence.

Quintilian detailed a complete educational program aimed at creating virtuous, well-rounded individuals who would contribute to their society. This concept of social responsibility became the heart of humanist education. As the great teacher Vittorino da Feltre explained, "Not everyone is called to be a physician, a lawyer, a philosopher, to live in the public eye, nor has everyone outstanding gifts of natural capacity, but all of us are created for the life of social duty, all are responsible for the personal influence that goes forth from us."

At his school in Mantua, Vittorino da Feltre produced several extraordinary pupils, including Lodovico Gonzaga and Federigo da Montefeltro, who became two of the most enlightened Renaissance rulers, and Lorenzo Valla, who became perhaps the most brilliant thinker of all the humanists. In 1440 Valla shocked the Church by proving that the Donation of Constantine was a forgery. This document allegedly passed control of the Western Roman Empire from the emperor Constantine to the papacy, giving the popes a legal basis for claims of political power. But by analyzing the style of Latin used in the manuscript, Valla proved that the document had been written long after Constantine's time.

Like most humanists, Valla did not question Christianity itself; nor did he question the pope's spiritual power—he simply believed that the pope should leave politics to the politicians, and he had the intellectual ammunition to prove it. Valla fled from Rome accused of heresy, but the humanist Pope Nicholas V later invited him back to help with a new phase of humanism: the translation of works from the ancient Greeks.

THE GREEK REVIVAL

After Manuel Chrysolorus laid the groundwork, Florentine humanists continued to pursue Greek culture. In 1423 a manuscript hunter returned from Greece with an incredible cache of 238 Greek manuscripts, and five years later, an Italian-born, Greek-speaking scholar became a professor at the University of Florence. Greek philosophy

LEON BATTISTA ALBERTI: THE UNIVERSAL MAN

As they strove to achieve the full potential of humanity, the humanists developed a new ideal they called the *uomo universale*, the universal man—a person who could do many things well. Today, when we describe someone as a *Renaissance man* or *Renaissance woman,* we are referring to this ideal. Many humanists were actively involved in politics and diplomacy while also writing on a wide range of subjects, but perhaps the greatest universal man of them all was Leon Battista Alberti.

Born in 1404 as the illegitimate, sickly child of a Florentine businessman, Alberti overcame his physical weakness by strenuous physical exercise, until he became one of the finest athletes of his time. He studied Latin and Greek, received a degree in law from the University of Bologna, and while still a student, wrote a Latin comedy in such perfect classical style that other scholars believed it was a long-lost manuscript. After graduating, Alberti took clerical positions in the Church, ultimately gaining an income that allowed him the freedom to pursue his wide-ranging interests.

was not completely new—in the Middle Ages, Aristotle was called "the master of those who know." But his ideas were studied in summaries and poor Latin translations. As the Florentines began to read Aristotle in the original Greek, they discovered that he did not believe in the immortality of the individual soul. For a people who were both Christians and individualists, this was deeply disturbing.

Between 1438 and 1445, a council was held—first in Ferrara and then in Florence—to unify the Christian churches of East and West. Although the council ended in failure, it brought many Greek scholars to Florence, including Gemistus Pletho, the greatest living authority on Plato, the philosopher who had been Aristotle's teacher. Plato believed in the immortal soul and presented his abstract philosophy in accessible, human dialogues. Gemistus apparently introduced Plato's

Along with satires and sonnets, Alberti wrote serious treatises on a dizzying array of subjects: family life, the judicial system, physics, mapmaking, mathematical puzzles, secret codes, rhetoric, Italian grammar, and horse breeding. More important, he wrote treatises on painting, sculpture, and architecture, describing the ideas that the great Renaissance artists were putting into practice. He was an accomplished musician who played the organ and wrote a variety of songs, and he designed machinery to try to raise a Roman galley from the bottom of a lake. On top of all this, he was one of the greatest architects of the age; when Pope Nicholas V decided to rebuild Rome, he commissioned Alberti to design a model city.

Alberti was so admired during his own lifetime that one contemporary said, "It is better to be silent about him than not to say enough." An anonymous reader scrawled a similar comment in the margin of one of Alberti's books: "Is there anything this man doesn't know?" But it is Alberti himself who best expresses the humanist ideal of the limitless potential of man: "Man is born not to mourn in idleness, but to work at magnificent and large-scale tasks, thereby pleasing and honoring God, and manifesting in himself perfect virtue, that is the fruit of happiness."

ideas to the ruler of Florence, Cosimo de' Medici, who hired a young Florentine named Marsilio Ficino to translate all of Plato's works into Latin, later giving him a house that became a center of humanist discussion known as the Platonic Academy. Though Aristotle continued to form the basis for university education, the humanist movement became more and more concerned with Plato and his abstract, spiritual ideas.

The interest in Greek led to interest in other languages and cultures as well. One member of the Platonic Academy, Giovanni Pico della Mirandola, tried to synthesize the great philosophies of many traditions—including Aristotle and Plato, Arab and Egyptian thinkers, Jewish mysticism, and Christianity—into a single great vision. In 1486 he published 900 theses (philosophic ideas) in Rome and invited other scholars to debate him. Pope Innocent VIII refused to allow the debate, and 13 of the theses were found to be heretical or dangerous. But Pico's *Oration on the Dignity of Man*, written as an introduction to the debate, marks the high point of the idealistic moral philosophy of humanism, centered on the infinite potential of human beings within the framework of God's will.

Pico begins by quoting an Arab passage: "There is nothing to be seen more wonderful than man." Later he imagines the creation, with God speaking to Adam:

> I have set you at the world's center that you may more easily observe whatever is in the world. I have made you neither of heaven nor of earth, neither mortal nor immortal, so that with freedom of choice and with honor, as though the maker and molder of yourself, you may fashion yourself in whatever shape you shall prefer. You shall have the power to degenerate into the lower forms of life, which are brutish. You shall have the power, out of your soul's judgment, to be reborn into the higher forms, which are divine.

Although Pico's lofty thinking was an exception, humanism had begun to lose its moral force by the late 15th century, as Platonists and non-Platonists argued over philosophical points and spent more time ridiculing each other than providing intellectual leadership. During the 16th century, philosophy developed in new directions, while humanism became more of a literary movement—aided by a great, new invention called the printing press.

PRINTING AND PRAGMATISM

The books that the early humanists loved so deeply were not books in the modern sense; they were handwritten manuscripts, copied in elegant, painstaking script, bound in expensive leather, and illustrated ("illuminated") with small, beautiful paintings. They were extremely expensive, and only wealthy people or scholars with wealthy patrons could afford them. An early Florentine humanist, Niccolò Niccoli, loved books so deeply that he sold off strips of farmland to buy them and died in bankruptcy. His wealthy friend Cosimo de' Medici paid

Niccolò's debts, rescued his books, and gave them to the people of Florence as the first public library in Europe.

The invention of the printing press in the mid-15th century changed the idea of a book, making inexpensive editions available to the middle class. At first, many humanists resisted printed books; the educated and enlightened duke of Urbino, Federigo da Montefeltro, refused to have printed books in his library. But by the end of the 15th century, printed books were carrying classical literature and humanist writings to a much larger audience—both in a geographic sense, as books circulated throughout Europe, and in an economic sense, as books became more common among the middle class. This led to translations of the classics into Italian, since many middle-class Italians could not read Latin.

Just as they had resisted printing, some humanists resisted the vernacular, believing that classical Latin and Greek were the only languages worthy of expressing great ideas. Lorenzo de' Medici added Hebrew to this list, and his own writing in Italian gained greater prestige for the Italian language. But even when scholars accepted Italian as a "worthy" language, it was the Italian of Dante, Petrarch, and Boccaccio, not the spoken Italian of the late Renaissance. Nonetheless, the more progressive writers expressed themselves in the Italian of their own time, and gradually Italian became the language of literature.

At the same time that printing and the Italian language were changing the literary world, Italy was thrown into political upheaval by foreign invasions. In 1513, amid this atmosphere of change, an out-of-work Florentine bureaucrat named Niccolò Machiavelli completed his most famous book, *The Prince*, written in powerful Italian prose. Although Machiavelli believed in the ideal of democracy, *The Prince* sets forth a very undemocratic, non-idealistic political philosophy that has been practiced by leaders since the beginning of human civilization: the end justifies the means. Discarding old questions of what is "right" or "good," Machiavelli tries to define what actually works in this imperfect world:

> . . . it appears to me more proper to go to the real truth of the matter than to its imagination; and many have imagined republics and principalities which have never been seen or known to exist in reality; for how we live is so far removed from how we ought to live, that he who abandons what is done for what ought to be

done, will rather learn to bring about his ruin than his preservation. A man who wishes to make a profession of goodness in everything must necessarily come to grief among so many who are not good. Therefore it is necessary for a prince, who wishes to maintain himself, to learn how not to be good, and to use this knowledge and not use it, according to the necessity of the case.

On a personal level, Machiavelli loved books and learning just as deeply as Petrarch had loved them almost two centuries earlier. But Machiavelli's brand of humanism was closer to the thinking of the 20th century than it was to the thinking of the 14th century. From the gentle scholarship of Petrarch, looking toward the distant past in order to understand the workings of his inner self, humanism had progressed to the cold, objective eye of Machiavelli, looking at the world in front of him, not to understand human potential, but simply to understand human politics.

CHAPTER 7 NOTES

pp. 69–70 "are so called . . ." and "The liberal arts owe . . ." Leonardo Bruni; quoted in Cronin. *The Florentine Renaissance,* (New York: E. P. Dutton, 1967) p. 53.

p. 70   "I truly believe . . ." Poggio Bracciolini; quoted in Cronin. pp. 48–49.

p. 71   "Not everyone is called . . ." Vittorino da Feltre; quoted in "Humanism," *Encyclopædia Brittanica,* vol. 20 (Chicago, 1991), p. 668.

p. 73   "It is better to be silent . . ." Politian; quoted in "Humanism," *Encyclopædia Brittanica,* p. 669.

p. 73   "Is there anything . . ." Anonymous; quoted in Cronin. *The Florentine Renaissance,* p. 87.

p. 73   "Man is born . . ." Leon Battista Alberti; quoted in Cronin, *The Florentine Renaissance,* p. 88.

p. 74   "I have set you . . ." Giovanni Pico della Mirandola, *Oration on the Dignity of Man;* excerpted in Werner L. Gundersheimer, ed. *The Italian Renaissance,* (Englewood Cliffs, NJ: Prentice Hall, 1965) p. 96. (Note: I have modernized the archaic "Thou shalt" form of God's speech without changing the meaning.)

p. 75   "it appears to me . . ." Niccolò Machiavelli, *The Prince,* Chapter XV; excerpted ibid., p. 124.

THE ART OF
THE EYE:

Painting, Sculpture, and Architecture

The Italian Renaissance was the age of the individual, a time when human beings clearly recognized their own importance and potential in the world. This naturally led to more realistic, objective observation of the human form and human behavior. Although the humanists expressed this philosophy eloquently in their writings, Renaissance individualism and realism found their greatest and most lasting representation in the visual arts.

The great age of art began in Florence in the early 15th century. But the roots of the artistic rebirth lie a century earlier, in the work of the Florentine painter Giotto, who lived from around 1267 to 1337. More than 200 years after Giotto's death, when the glory of Renaissance art had already begun to fade, the artist and art historian Giorgio Vasari wrote: "Giotto alone, in a rude and inept age, when all good methods of art had long been lost, dead and buried in the ruins of war, set art upon the path that may be called the true one."

This is a slight exaggeration, for other artists were also breaking away from the flat, rigid style of the Middle Ages. But Giotto was the towering artistic genius of the 14th century, so far ahead of his time that no other painter approached his level of work for almost a hundred years. Although he lacked the knowledge of perspective, Giotto used space, light, and color to create a powerful sense of the human form, and he had a storyteller's ability to capture the essential moment in a particular scene. This quality is especially strong in the fresco paintings for the Arena Chapel in Padua, which portray a series of scenes from the life of Christ. In the scene showing the kiss of Judas as he betrays Jesus, the betrayal seems to hover in the air between the two men.

For almost a century after Giotto, painters were content to sign themselves "disciple of Giotto, the good master." It was not until the second decade of the 15th century that a new master arose to take his place.

THE EARLY FIFTEENTH CENTURY

The two great breakthroughs in the development of Renaissance art were the rediscovery of classical Greco-Roman style and the rediscovery of mathematical or "artificial" perspective, which allows a painter to represent three-dimensional reality on a two-dimensional plane. The man behind both of these breakthroughs was the Florentine architect Filippo Brunelleschi, whose work amid the ruins of Rome is discussed in the box feature of Chapter 3. Brunelleschi's most famous accomplishment, the dome of the Florence cathedral, was based more on Byzantine domes than on Roman style. However, in his designs for other buildings, he adopted the simple, well-proportioned elegance and slender columns of classical architecture, along with graceful, circular Romanesque arches, to mark a clear departure from the angular, ornate style of Gothic architecture.

It's unclear exactly how Brunelleschi discovered perspective, but it apparently emerged out of his observations of ancient Roman buildings, along with readings of a classical text on architecture and some knowledge of Arab mathematics. Simply put, perspective depends on a "vanishing point" toward which all lines that seem to go "into" the picture converge. Thus, objects that are supposed to be farther away from the viewer appear smaller, while those that are closer appear larger. Perspective modifies geometric structure, since there are no true right angles.

Brunelleschi used perspective in his architectural designs and demonstrated the technique to other Florentine artists, including Masaccio, who became the most influential painter since Giotto. Though he died at the age of 27 in 1428, Masaccio not only mastered perspective but also established two other techniques that became essential aspects of Italian painting: the portrayal of human anatomy under loose, drapelike clothing, and a way of painting shadows, called *chiaroscuro*, that creates a sense of light within the darkness.

In his masterpiece, *The Tribute Money*—which shows Jesus sending Peter off to find tax money in the mouth of a fish—Masaccio combined all of these techniques with classical forms and a clear eye to create a more powerful sense of reality than anything ever painted before. His figures stand firmly on the ground in three-dimensional space, and they seem to think and gesture as real human beings. More than half a century later, Leonardo da Vinci wrote, "After [Giotto] this art declined again, because everyone imitated the pictures that were already done . . . until Masaccio showed by his perfect works how those who take for their standard anyone but nature—the mistress of all masters—weary themselves in vain."

Sculpture is less concerned with perspective, because it is itself a three-dimensional medium. However, much of early Renaissance sculpture was not freestanding statues but rather shallow reliefs designed to adorn doors, altars, or buildings. The new understanding of perspective made these reliefs come alive. The Florentine sculptor Lorenzo Ghiberti demonstrated this in his second set of bronze doors for the Baptistery, which Michelangelo thought fit to stand at the Gates of Paradise.

The most important and original sculptor of the period was Brunelleschi's younger friend, Donatello, who had accompanied him to Rome. Although inspired by classical style, Donatello brought his own uniquely human vision to his work. His early marble statues of *St. Mark* and *St. George*, completed by 1415, set a new standard for simple, powerful realism, while his later bronze statue of *David*, completed for Cosimo de' Medici around 1442, was the first large, freestanding nude since the days of ancient Rome. Combining the Greek celebration of

THE ROLE OF THE ARTIST

During the early Renaissance, the artist occupied a humble position in society. He was required to belong to one of the craftsmen's guilds and to function within a workshop system, in which a master and his apprentices would turn out a wide variety of pieces—from painted jewelry boxes to religious frescoes—to the exact specifications of the patron or guild that was paying for the work. Even a great painter like Giotto, who was famous throughout Italy, was subject to these limitations. The guild requirement continued throughout the Renaissance, but during the 15th century, as the quality of art developed, the role and status of the artist developed as well.

Filippo Brunelleschi was apparently the first artist to demand a new level of recognition for his individual genius. According to one early biographer, Brunelleschi refused to split the commission for the Baptistery doors with his competitor Lorenzo Ghiberti and stalked off to Rome to become an architect. Later he reluctantly agreed to share the commission for the cathedral dome with Ghiberti, but he feigned an illness at a crucial stage in the building to make it clear who was doing the real work. Brunelleschi was awarded a bonus of 100 florins as the "inventor" of the dome—a word that had not been used to describe an artist since the days of ancient Rome.

In his treatise on painting, Leon Battista Alberti raised the status of the artist by making it clear that painting depended on an understanding of complex mathematical and philosophical problems as well as on manual skill. At about the same time, Cosimo de' Medici set a new standard for art patronage by treating the artists who worked for him with respect for their talent and individuality. He became close friends with Donatello and supported him with a pension in his old age. At

the human body with Renaissance religious piety, its youthful grace seems to represent the youthful spirit of the Renaissance itself. Perhaps most startling of all, it was created not to adorn a church, but to decorate a private home: the Palazzo Medici.

the same time, he put up with the wild lusts of Filippo Lippi, who would drop his brushes to chase after beautiful women and disappear for days at a time.

Patrons in other cities were not always so understanding. When Paolo Uccello worked in a monastery in Rome, he ran away because the abbot fed him nothing but cheese. "If he'd gone on any more," the artist said, "I wouldn't be Paolo Uccello, I'd be pure cheese." When Leonardo da Vinci painted *The Last Supper* on a convent wall in Milan, the prior complained that he spent half a day just looking at the painting, to which Leonardo replied, "Men of genius sometimes accomplish most when they work least." Of course, the prior wasn't paying for Leonardo's time; his wealthy patron, Lodovico Sforza, made sure that Leonardo lived well during his stay in Milan.

Michelangelo further raised the status of the artist by the sheer power of his genius. He was called "divine" in his own time, and later in his life he was wealthy enough to work on the dome of St. Peter's without pay. Even more significantly, Pope Julius II allowed him complete freedom in choosing the subject matter and designing the ceiling of the Sistine Chapel. Raphael, Titian, and the architect Donato Bramante all became wealthy from their work, and Titian was knighted by the Holy Roman Emperor Charles V and accepted in the highest levels of society.

In 1563 Michelangelo and the grand duke of Florence, Cosimo I—a descendant of the original Cosimo de' Medici—founded the first European academy of art, where artists could meet as gentlemen and philosophers to discuss their work. Eight years later, Florence dropped the requirement that an artist must belong to a guild. From his beginnings as a humble craftsman, the Renaissance artist had come a long way.

DEVELOPMENT AND EXPERIMENT: 1430–1500

By the time that Donatello completed his statue of *David*, the rest of Italy had begun to notice the work of the Florentine artists. The humanist Leon Battista Alberti, who had been born during his father's

By the time of this portrait around 1485, painters had mastered realistic portrayal of the human form. Although officially credited to Filippino Lippi, son of Filippo Lippi, some art historians think this portrait was painted by Sandro Botticelli, in whose workshop the younger Lippi studied. (Fillippino Lippi, *Portrait of a Youth*, Andrew W. Mellon Collection, ©1994 National Gallery of Art, Washington)

exile from Florence, visited the city during the 1430s and was struck by the artistic genius displayed by Brunelleschi, Masaccio, Donatello, and Ghiberti. In 1436 Alberti wrote a treatise in Italian on painting, in which he described mathematical perspective and discussed other issues of composition, technique, and subject matter. Alberti's work, along with actual observation of Florentine art, inspired several generations of artists who mastered perspective and experimented with different techniques of representing reality.

Some painters became obsessed with perspective, as though it were a new toy. Paolo Uccello sat up all night at his drawing table, murmuring, "Oh, what a delightful thing is this perspective!" On the other hand, the pious monk Fra Angelico used perspective almost casually to make his deeply religious scenes more real and powerful. The not-so-pious ex-monk Filippo Lippi moved away from Masaccio's simple yet serious figures to a lighter, more complex style. Perhaps the greatest of this second generation was Domenico Veneziano, who combined a sophisticated use of perspective with a delicate sense of light in his masterpiece, the *St. Lucy Altarpiece.*

The generation that followed made greater breakthroughs. Veneziano's assistant, Piero della Francesca, took perspective to its highest level and developed a fine eye for light and color, creating accurate landscapes and human figures of such simplicity and stillness that they seem suspended in time. Piero wrote the first full treatise on the system of perspective, which allowed artists of lesser talent to represent reality accurately. The Paduan master Andrea Mantegna experimented with the extremes of perspective, painting a disturbing, foreshortened figure of the dead Christ as if the viewer were standing at the foot of the corpse.

Although much of Renaissance art was still religious, wealthy patrons began commissioning art for their own homes, and artists began to experiment with subject matter. Mantegna portrayed the Gonzaga family in their court at Mantua, and Mino da Fiesole sculpted a realistic likeness of Piero de' Medici—the first portrait bust since the fall of Rome. Lorenzo de' Medici's favorite painter, Sandro Botticelli, created exquisite, sensual scenes from Greek and Roman mythology, and produced strange allegories that combined medieval ideas with Renaissance realism. The eccentric Piero di Cosimo stretched the limits of subject matter even further, painting a series of scenes from early human life.

In their attempt to represent reality, artists of the later 15th century became more concerned with human anatomy and motion. Antonio del Pollaiuolo created movement in his paintings with strong lines and bold brush strokes, while his small bronze of *Hercules and Antaeus* shows the two heroes wrestling, with every muscle clearly defined. Andrea del Verrocchio, in his huge bronze equestrian statue of the condottiere Colleoni, contrasted the massive yet detailed forms of horse and armor with the bulging eyes of the soldier, ready for action. In *The Last Judgment,* Luca Signorelli painted powerfully muscled demons, twisting and turning in a flurry of motion.

Throughout most of Italy, the preferred form of wall painting was the fresco, in which water-based paint is applied to wet plaster. Panel paintings were usually water-based paint on wood—or later on canvas. The artists of Flanders in northern Europe, who were experiencing their own artistic Renaissance, pioneered the use of oil-based paints, and there was contact between Italian and Flemish artists as early as the 1430s. But it was not until the last quarter of the 15th century that the great Venetian artist Giovanni Bellini developed oil painting into a distinct Italian style. Bellini used oils to create a glowing, lustrous sense of light and color, while also showing the influence of the Flemish interest in detailed landscapes. Bellini's style was further developed by his pupils, Giorgione and Titian, who both concentrated less on land-scapes and more on people.

In architecture, Leon Battista Alberti—who did so much to spread the ideas of Renaissance painting—followed in the footsteps of Brunelleschi by applying classical ideals of proportion and natural simplicity. Whereas medieval architects had designed churches to be imposing reminders of God's awesome power, Alberti designed them as places of pleasurable retreat and meditation. "And if it is true," he asked, "as people say, that pleasure is to be found in a place where our senses receive all they demand of nature, who will hesitate to call a church a nest of pleasure?"

When Alberti speaks of nature, he is not referring to forests or mountains, but rather to the natural reality of human life. In the final stage of Renaissance art, called the High Renaissance, the relationship

*St. Francis in the Desert, a panel painted around 1480 by Giovanni Bellini, demon-
strates the Venetian technique of using oil paint to create a glowing sense of light, as
well as the typical Renaissance use of symbolic details in the landscape.* (Copyright
The Frick Collection, New York)

of art and nature reached its highest form of expression. And it began
with another "universal man"—like Alberti, a man who could do most
things well and many things brilliantly—a man named Leonardo da
Vinci.

THE HIGH RENAISSANCE

Leonardo da Vinci, born the illegitimate son of a Florentine notary in
1452, studied in the workshop of Andrea del Verrocchio and was
accepted as a master in the painter's guild at the age of 20. A genius of
incredibly varied interests, Leonardo filled some 5,000 pages with
sketches and notes on subjects ranging from painting and perspective
to military fortifications and the possibilities of human flight. With his

restless mind, Leonardo left many of his great projects unfinished, and his reputation as an artist rests on his drawings and a small number of paintings, including his most famous works: *The Last Supper,* a fresco completed in Milan in 1498, and the *Mona Lisa,* painted in Florence in the early 1500s.

Leonardo developed the technical skills of drawing and painting to such a high level that he was able to move beyond the earlier Renaissance concern with representing the physical reality of the human form and concentrate on representing the personality within the form. "Paint the face," he explained, "in such a way that it will be easy to understand what is going on in the mind." In the *Mona Lisa,* he took this even further, painting his subject's famous smile with such intriguing mystery that people have wondered for almost 500 years exactly what *was* going on in her mind.

Leonardo was an original thinker who emphasized that the artist must take life itself as his master, rather than the works of previous artists. He was not interested in rediscovering the art or thought of Rome and Greece; nor did he wish to copy Giotto or Masaccio—he was interested in discovering his own human nature and the nature of those around him. "The painter will produce pictures of little merit if he takes the works of others as his standard; but if he will apply himself to learn from the objects of nature, he will produce good results."

Leonardo marked a transition from the classical concerns of the earlier Renaissance to the original genius of the High Renaissance. But it was a younger Florentine, Michelangelo Buonarroti, who brought that original genius to its full potential. Born in 1475, Michelangelo came from a proud but poor noble family, and his father resisted his son's artistic ambitions. Yet even as a young man, Michelangelo exhibited a strength of character that few could resist for long. Like Leonardo, he was a man of many talents: sculptor, painter, architect, and poet. But he had a more focused genius than Leonardo. Perhaps more than any individual in human history, Michelangelo's life and work define what it means to be an artist.

Like the works of most 15th century sculptors, Michelangelo's early works are skillful copies of classical style—so skillful in fact that a clever art dealer buried one of his statues in a vineyard and sold it as a newly discovered antique. However, he soon moved beyond imitation. In the

Pietà, completed in Rome in 1499, he took a medieval Gothic motif of the dead Christ stretched across Mary's lap and transformed it with the pure physical and spiritual beauty of the figures. Art historian Kenneth Clark calls the *Pietà* "a new stretch of the imagination, for he has achieved what theorists tell us is impossible, a perfect fusion of Gothic and Classical art." Michelangelo's monumental, muscular figure of *David,* completed in Florence in 1504, seems to represent the confident maturity of the High Renaissance as surely as Donatello's slender, youthful *David* represented the optimism of the early Renaissance.

Michelangelo's greatest achievements as a painter are his biblical scenes on the ceiling of the Sistine Chapel, completed in 1512, and his huge fresco of *The Last Judgment* on the altar wall of the chapel, completed much later, in 1541. In these paintings, as in his later sculptures, he demonstrates a fascination with large, powerful, naked human forms, going beyond nature to create godlike and demonlike heroes struggling with the harsh reality of their destiny. In one of his sonnets, Michelangelo expressed his vision of art's timeless power:

> Shapes that seem alive,
> Wrought in hard mountain marble, will survive
> Their maker, whom the years to dust return!
> . . . Art hath her turn
> And triumphs over Nature.

Beginning in 1508, Michelangelo had to compete for papal patronage with a young painter named Raphael. Though he did not have the universal genius of Leonardo and Michelangelo, Raphael was perhaps the finest pure painter of the High Renaissance. He borrowed ideas from both Leonardo and Michelangelo, but expressed them in his own confidently graceful style. His series of frescoes in the rooms of the Vatican represent a perfect union of pagan and Christian themes, while his study of Pope Julius II redefined the art of the portrait, portraying the aged warrior-pope with downcast eyes that seem to ponder the weight of this world and the promise of the world to come.

The fourth great artist of the High Renaissance, Titian, made portrait painting his specialty, although he was also masterful in his treatment of religious and mythological scenes. Working in the Venetian

Michelangelo's David. *In this older photo, the sculpture still wears the fig leaf added by a later artist, reflecting the strict morality in Italy after the Renaissance. Today* David *is once again as Michelangelo created him.* (Original sculpture Galleria dell'Accademia, Florence; photo courtesy Library of Congress)

THE ITALIAN RENAISSANCE

style of oil painting, Titian combined the control of color and light exhibited by earlier Venetian painters with the powerful representation of human form developed by Michelangelo and Raphael. His abilities made him the wealthiest and most famous artist up to that time—so much in demand that there was "hardly a noble of high rank, scarcely a prince or a lady of great name whose portrait has not been painted by Titian."

Raphael died at the age of 37 in 1520, but Michelangelo and Titian both lived long, productive lives that carried them beyond the great age of Renaissance art. By the time of Michelangelo's death in 1564 and Titian's death in 1576, a new style called Mannerism dominated the Italian artistic world. Michelangelo himself pointed the way toward the new direction, as he exaggerated human figures in his search for a more powerful reality beyond the imitation of Nature. But as artists continued to experiment with the limits of form and structure, often relying more on technical displays than on clear vision, Mannerism marked a decline in the close relationship between the reality of human life and the reality of art. It was still fine art, and it could still excite the emotions and dazzle the senses. But it was no longer the art of the Renaissance.

CHAPTER 8 NOTES

p. 77   "Giotto alone . . ." Giorgio Vasari, *Lives of the Most Excellent Italian Architects, Painters, and Sculptors;* quoted in *Horizon Book*, p. 33.

p. 79   "After this art declined . . ." Leonardo da Vinci; quoted in Hale, p. 98.

p. 81   "If he'd gone on . . ." Paolo Uccello; quoted in Cronin, *The Florentine Renaissance*, p. 159.

p. 81   "Men of genius . . ." Leonardo da Vinci; quoted in Cronin, *The Florentine Renaissance*, p. 166.

p. 83   "Oh, what a delightful thing . . ." Paolo Uccello; quoted in Hale, p. 98.

p. 84   "And if it is true . . ." Leon Battista Alberti; quoted in Cronin, *The Florentine Renaissance*, p. 88.

p. 86   "Paint the face . . ." Leonardo da Vinci; quoted in *Horizon Book*, p. 122.

p. 86   "The painter will produce . . ." Leonardo da Vinci, quoted in Gundersheimer, p. 179.

p. 87   "a new stretch of the imagination . . ." Kenneth Clark, "The Young Michelangelo," in *Horizon Book*, p. 109.

p. 87   "Shapes that seem alive . . ." Michelangelo sonnet; quoted in Kenneth Clark, "The Young Michelangelo" p. 112.

p. 89   "hardly a noble . . ." Vasari, *Lives;* quoted in *Horizon Book*, p. 297.

SCIENCE AND TECHNOLOGY:

Observation and Experiment

Although we often think of the Renaissance as the beginning of the modern world, it was not at all modern when viewed in the light of 20th-century science. Princes, popes, and generals depended on astrology to decide their actions, while diseases were blamed on God's wrath, the stars, or an imbalance of the four humors. Alchemists tried to turn base metals into gold, and apothecaries mixed potions that did more to harm the patient than the disease did. At the beginning of the Renaissance, many people still believed the world was flat, and even by the end of the period, most believed that the sun revolved around the Earth.

Gradually, however, Renaissance thinkers groped their way out of the darkness toward new theories and knowledge based on scientific evidence. They were aided in their quest by rediscovered manuscripts from the ancient Greeks, but these could be as much a hindrance as a help. The most powerful Renaissance writers and artists—men like Machiavelli and Michelangelo—were those who broke away from classical ideas and relied on their own thinking and seeing. The same is true of the scientists; and the most important breakthroughs occurred in the later Renaissance, when they began to go beyond their classical models and rely on the evidence of their eyes.

THE WORK OF LEONARDO DA VINCI

The man who symbolized this new direction more than any other single human being was Leonardo da Vinci. In his art, Leonardo always painted or drew what his own eyes could actually see, rather than following the work of others. He brought this same attitude to his scientific work, which he meticulously recorded in his notebooks—filling thousands of pages with accurate sketches of everything from human anatomy to military machinery. "What I say is borne out by experience," he wrote on one page, neatly summing up the modern scientific method.

Most of Leonardo's scientific investigations began with his artistic desire to reproduce nature as accurately as possible. In order to better portray the human form, he dissected more than 30 cadavers, until Pope Leo X banned him from the mortuary in Rome. Leonardo was not the first artist to dissect dead bodies—Antonio Pollaiuolo had done it before him—but Leonardo did it with such thoroughness and care that his drawings of tiny blood vessels match perfectly with modern X rays. Leonardo also studied the anatomy of the horse in order to portray horses more realistically in equestrian statues.

Blessed with almost superhuman eyesight, Leonardo observed the flight of birds more accurately than anyone had ever observed it before. This in turn led him to consider the possibility of human flight:

A bird is an instrument working according to mathematical law, which instrument it is within the capacity of man to reproduce with all its movements, but not with a corresponding degree of strength. . . . We may therefore say that such an instrument constructed by man is lacking in nothing except the life of the bird, and this life must needs be supplied from that of man.

Leonardo designed many flying machines, including a helicopter that would have flown if he had had an appropriate power source. All

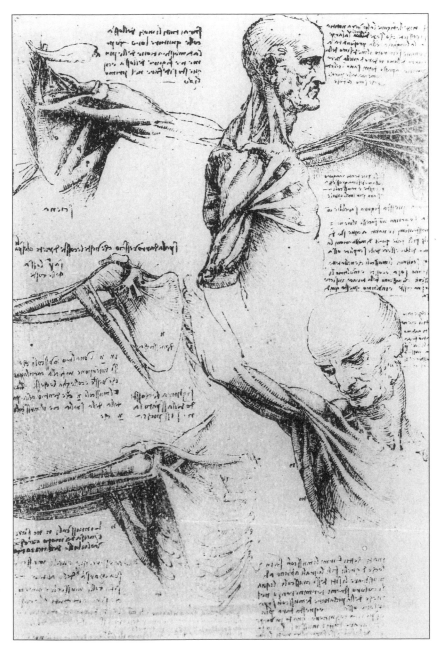

A sketch of the muscles of the shoulder by Leonardo da Vinci, based on careful dissections. (Original in the Royal Library, Windsor; reproduced in Vasari, *Leonardo da Vinci,* Florence; General Collections, Library of Congress)

he needed was the internal combustion engine, which wasn't invented for another 400 years.

Leonardo's flying machines—as well as his designs for parachutes, tanks, and automobiles—were what he called "pre- imagining," or "the imagining of things that are to be." But he also engaged in more down-to-earth scientific and technical thinking. He developed topographical maps that aided in irrigation and flood prevention, and he designed a new type of gate for a canal in Milan. He studied the flight of projectiles and designed fortifications and weapons, including several machine guns. He made extensive, accurate observations about light and optics, designed the first telescope, and created a test to determine the quality of mirrors. He designed an incredible variety of machines, from needle-sharpeners and weaving looms to paddle-wheels and roasting spits.

A few of Leonardo's designs, such as his canal gate, were actually produced during his lifetime, but he never published his notebooks and most of his work was not understood until long after the Renaissance was over. Thus it's difficult to know how much influence Leonardo had on other scientists of the time. However, as historian Peter Laven points out, Leonardo worked in the intellectual circles of Florence and Milan, he had a reputation as a great talker, and he collaborated with other thinkers on several projects. Thus, Laven believes we can assume "that his ideas were familiar to the scientific environment in which he found himself . . . the likelihood is that Leonardo's thought was an important landmark in the development of scientific ideas."

MATHEMATICS—EARTHLY AND OTHERWISE

Mathematics had meaning on several levels for the people of the Renaissance. On the one hand, it could be a practical tool used in business—the merchants of Florence replaced cumbersome Roman numerals with more efficient Arabic numerals and developed modern methods of keeping business records and accounts. On the other hand, mathematics could have mystical, magical meanings used in astrology and other methods of predicting the future. On an even higher level, to the followers of Plato, mathematics represented the overall harmony and structure of the universe.

One of the most down-to-earth mathematicians was Fra Luca Pacioli, a Franciscan monk who was fascinated by the new theories of perspective developed by Renaissance artists. Pacioli wanted to apply these geometric ideas to everyday life, and in 1494 he published a long volume entitled *Summary of Arithmetic, Geometry, Proportion and Proportionality*, which laid the foundation for the modern study of mathematics. Much of this work is devoted to practical subjects, including the system of double-entry bookkeeping still used by accountants today. In 1509 Pacioli published a more advanced volume on perspective and solid forms entitled *Of Divine Proportion*, with illustrations by Leonardo da Vinci.

While the study of perspective—along with translations of the Greek geometer Euclid—led to advances in geometry, Renaissance mathematicians also made important contributions to algebra. Pacioli is often credited with discovering the square root, and Italian mathematicians of the mid-16th century discovered a solution to third-degree equations (equations involving numbers to the third power). It's unclear exactly who made this breakthrough, since several leading mathematicians charged each other with plagiarism. However, it's typical of the times that one of the men who published the solution, Girolamo Cardano, also wrote a book on natural magic in which he tried to explain phenomena such as magnetism and weather with a strange mixture of science and superstition.

Perhaps the greatest scientific breakthrough during the Renaissance was in astronomy. Ironically, the widespread belief in astrology actually led to more accurate observation of the stars, as did the more sophisticated navigation methods needed to guide ships across the ocean. At the same time, the old Julian calendar had fallen out of sync with the reality of the solar year, and efforts to reform the calendar began during the reign of Sixtus IV (1471–84). This led to a century of observations as astronomers tried to gather enough data to produce an accurate calendar—a process that culminated in the Gregorian calendar at the end of the 16th century.

Despite these practical concerns, early Renaissance thinkers operated from theories first and observations second. At the beginning of the Renaissance, most scientific theories were based on Aristotle, who believed that the Earth was the center of the universe. However, after the philosophy of Plato and his later followers (Neo-Platonists) was introduced in the mid-15th century, some thinkers began to take a new approach. Plato believed that the universe was unified by a sort of cosmic mathematics, and the Neo-Platonists took this even further into the realm of mysticism and magic. As Renaissance philosophers considered these ideas, they began to see the universe in more expansive, abstract terms.

Nicholas of Cusa, a German philosopher who spent many years in Italy working for the Church, connected the infinite nature of God with the infinite nature of mathematics and the universe. And if the universe was infinite, then one point was no more the center than another point. At the University of Bologna, Domenico Maria da Novara was also influenced by these mystical mathematical ideas, but unlike Nicholas of Cusa, he backed up his philosophy with careful observation of the heavens—aided by a visiting Polish astronomer named Nicolaus Copernicus. Copernicus apparently developed his theory that the Earth revolved around the sun during his stay in Italy, but he didn't publish it until just before his death in 1543, for fear of being charged with heresy by the Church. By that time, the concept of a sun-centered system had been circulating among Italian intellectuals for 30 years.

MEDICAL SCIENCE

The Renaissance was not a good time to be sick. New, more virulent diseases attacked the population, brought to Europe by trade with Asia and America. Physicians bled their patients with leeches and argued whether it was better to perform surgery with a knife or a red-hot metal cautery. Apothecaries mixed strange, deadly potions, and doctors tried desperate cures without understanding what they were doing. When Lorenzo de' Medici suffered from intestinal problems, his physicians fed him crushed pearls, which probably caused his death. When Pope Innocent VIII lay dying, his physicians gave him a blood transfusion from three 10-year-old boys, which didn't save the pope and killed all three boys.

Despite this poor medical care, the Italian Renaissance set the stage for modern medicine and public health practices. When the Black Death devastated Florence in 1348, the writer Giovanni Boccaccio— who described the actual symptoms of the plague with bone-chilling realism—claimed that the epidemic "started in the East either through the influence of the heavenly bodies or because God's just anger with our wicked deeds sent it as a punishment to mortal men." But 50 years later, wealthy Florentines understood the direct relationship between filth and disease, as well as the concept of quarantining infected individuals. Venice and Genoa pioneered the practice of quarantining ships around the same time, and Venice tried unsuccessfully to keep malaria-breeding rice paddies away from the city. Many cities built public hospitals throughout the 15th and 16th centuries.

During the height of Renaissance culture, the most disturbing epidemic was syphilis, a sexually transmitted disease that was apparently brought to Europe by sailors who had accompanied Columbus on his first voyage to the New World. The epidemic broke out in Naples during the French invasion of 1495 and was dubbed the "love pestilence" or the "French sickness" as it spread throughout Italy. In 1535 a brilliant physician from Verona named Girolamo Fracastoro published a long Latin poem in which he identified the causes, symptoms, and treatments for the disease, and—in typical Renaissance style—named it after a figure from Greek mythology. Fracastoro went on to become an expert on infectious diseases.

Renaissance doctors and apothecaries followed the tradition of herbal medicine practiced throughout the Middle Ages, and the rediscovery of Greek medical texts introduced many new plants with potential healing powers. However, serious problems arose because of misidentification of plants and misunderstanding of their specific healing properties. In 1533 the Venetian Senate established a chair at the University of Padua for the study of herbal medicines, and they later added an herb garden to provide teachers and students with a ready supply of plants to investigate—an important step in developing a more modern, scientific approach to medicine.

Although artists like Leonardo da Vinci and Antonio del Pollaiuolo studied anatomy with great care and precision, they were not interested in healing people, but rather in portraying the human form. Throughout the 15th and early 16th centuries, the supreme authority on human anatomy was the 2nd-century Greek physician Galen, who had based his studies on dissections of Barbary apes. The modern science of anatomy began with Andreas Vesalius, a surgeon and teacher at the

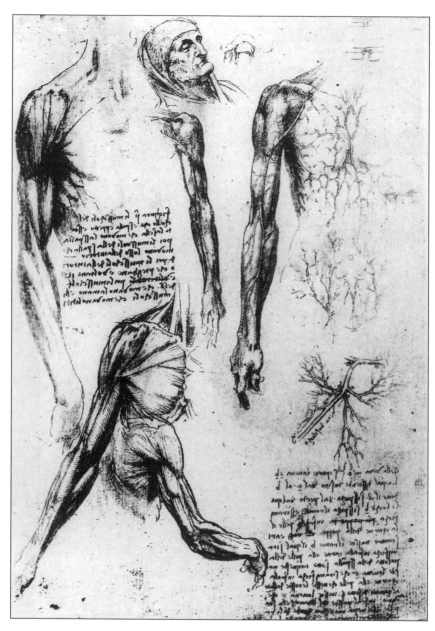

Careful dissection of human cadavers during the Renaissance led to more accurate understanding of anatomy. (Sketch by Leonardo da Vinci; original in the Royal Library, Windsor; reproduced in Vasari, *Leonardo da Vinci,* Florence; General Collections, Library of Congress)

University of Padua who dissected dozens of cadavers and collected bones from graveyards, gallows, and mortuaries. In 1543 Vesalius published his findings in a comprehensive volume entitled *On the Fabric of the Human Body,* illustrated with detailed woodcuts. At first other physicians were outraged by his ideas, but Vesalius won over his critics, performing popular, hands-on demonstrations at three different universities—so popular in fact that the operating theater at the University of Pisa collapsed under the weight of the audience.

TECHNOLOGY

On a philosophical level, the scientists of the late Renaissance took a giant step away from the Middle Ages by relying on their own observations rather than on accepted authorities. On a more practical level, Renaissance inventors and engineers did not have to make this kind of breakthrough because the Middle Ages had been a time of substantial technical achievement, including huge cathedrals, shipbuilding, canals and dikes, windmills, waterwheels, textile machinery, glass production, the magnetic compass, and the discovery of gunpowder. The technology of the Italian Renaissance focused on developing and refining these earlier achievements to new heights.

Irrigation and drainage projects were completed on a larger scale than before, and the wealthy Venetians changed the course of rivers. The rebuilding of Rome—originally conceived by Leon Battista Alberti—was an enormous effort of city planning, including widening streets and building bridges as well as the huge construction project of St. Peter's. Brunelleschi's earlier dome for the Florence cathedral was as much a technical achievement as an artistic one, and he designed new machinery to lift heavy stones into place. Military machinery and fortifications were a constant concern throughout the Renaissance, although the artists who often designed them—including Leonardo and Michelangelo—worked more from imagination and theory than from practical military experience.

The Venetians pioneered mass-production techniques in their shipbuilding arsenal and glass industry, while Leonardo invented a machine called a "gig-mill" that mechanically lifted the nap of textiles, thereby replacing a whole class of unskilled workers. The mill was so effective that the English Parliament outlawed it in 1551, and workers rioted when it was first used extensively during the Industrial Revolution. Renaissance inventors were especially intrigued by machines that transmitted power through gears and cranks. They applied this technology not only to serious manufacturing and construction machinery but also to fanciful machinery for theatrical displays and to a "book wheel" that allowed scholars to study many books at a time.

The most important technological breakthrough of the Renaissance period was the printing press using movable type, developed by the German Johann Gutenberg during the mid-15th century. The Italians quickly adopted the new technology, and by the end of the century, Venice was the largest printing center in the world. Italian techniques of casting metal type were used for the next 300 years. The Italians also made other breakthroughs in the casting and refining of metals, developing new acids and alloys and building more powerful furnaces. This interest in metal technology reflected three great concerns of the Italian Renaissance: learning, art, and war. Movable type, bronze statues, and other art objects all required sophisticated metal work; so did guns and cannons.

CHAPTER 9 NOTES

p. 92   "What I say . . ." Leonardo da Vinci; quoted in Peter Ritchie-Calder. *Leonardo & the Age of the Eye* (New York: Simon & Schuster, 1970), p. 58.

p. 92   "A bird is an instrument . . ." Leonardo da Vinci; quoted in Bronowski. "Leonardo da Vinci," in *Horizon Book*, pp. 186-87.

p. 94   "that his ideas were familiar . . ." Peter Laven. *Renaissance Italy: 1454–1534* (New York: G. P. Putnam's Sons, 1966), pp. 174-75.

p. 97   "started in the East . . ." Giovanni Boccaccio, *The Decameron;* in Aldington, trans. p. 30

RENAISSANCE LIFE:

Men and Women in a Changing World

The Renaissance was an age of youth. In 1427 almost half the people of Tuscany were under 20 years of age, and during most of the period, the average life expectancy at birth was less than 30 years. This average was greatly influenced by the high rate of death in childhood, but nonetheless the people of the Renaissance grew up fast. Boys might be apprenticed to learn a trade by the age of seven, while girls destined for the religious life would enter a nunnery at 12. Young men could vote in Florence at 14, and they began to pay taxes and serve in the military at 18. Although men usually married later in life, when they were more financially secure, women married in their mid-teens, and an unmarried woman of 20 was considered an old maid.

With the prospect of a short life before them, men sought their fortunes at an early age. Ghiberti and Brunelleschi were in their early twenties when they competed to design the Baptistery doors, and Donatello was only 17 when he accompanied Brunelleschi to Rome.

Masaccio, the most important painter of the early Renaissance, died at the age of 27. Lorenzo de' Medici became "first citizen" of Florence at 20 and died at 43. His son, Giovanni, became a cardinal at 13 and pope at 37. The philosopher Pico della Mirandola tried to synthesize the knowledge of the world at the age of 23 and died at 31.

There was no concept of middle age, and Michelangelo considered himself an old man at the age of 42—although he actually lived to the ripe old age of 89. Other men and women lived long, fruitful lives as well. Titian was still painting at 90, Cosimo de' Medici dominated Florence at 75, and Isabella d'Este remained the grand dame of Renaissance culture into her sixties. On the other hand, her sister, Beatrice, died in childbirth at the age of 21—a common fate for Renaissance women. Older people were respected for their wisdom, and Venice in particular placed its faith in experience. Unlike youthful Florence, Venice did not allow men to vote until the age of 25, and the average age of the doges who served as head of state was over 70.

Concepts of human life evolved during the Renaissance, as people developed new ideals for men, women, and their relationship in marriage. These changing ideals were most important for the upper class, who could afford to live their lives based on philosophical ideas. But they also affected the middle class, who tended to copy the wealthy in their manners and attitudes. We know less about the lower class, but for the vast majority of peasants and day laborers, life was probably as hard as it had always been, a dreary cycle of birth, work, and death, with a few joyous moments of family and festival to elevate the spirit.

THE IDEAL MAN

During the early Renaissance, the ideal man was the sober, sensible merchant, who dressed in simple, monklike clothing, conducted his business honestly, worshipped God piously, and took good care of his family. He was expected to be thrifty and moderate in his personal affairs, but generous and public-spirited in the affairs of his city. In the mid-15th century, the wealthy Cosimo de' Medici still followed this ideal, living in apparent simplicity, always careful to minimize his private fortune, while ostentatiously advertising his generosity to the city of Florence.

Gradually, however, the upper class became more open in displaying their wealth. They wore outrageously expensive clothing, built luxurious palaces and villas, and put on parties that involved full theatrical productions. To celebrate his marriage to a Roman noblewoman, Lorenzo de' Medici convinced his father to hold a knightly tournament in the style of northern Europe—a grand spectacle seldom seen in Florence. Pope Sixtus IV gave banquets with mountains of exotic food served on silver dishes adorned with full-sized figures from mythology. Isabella d'Este considered her husband's clothing to be so important that she pawned her jewels in order to buy him rich, new garments for a diplomatic mission to Milan.

As the earlier ideal of simplicity faded, another ideal emerged that had little to do with issues of wealth or business, but rather reflected the great age of art and humanism. This was the *uomo universale,* the universal man who could do all things well. Leon Battista Alberti and Leonardo da Vinci were the most astonishing embodiments of this ideal, but many others also excelled in a variety of fields. Rulers like Federigo da Montefeltro and Lorenzo de' Medici demonstrated brilliance in scholarship and poetry, while poets and scholars demonstrated brilliance in politics and diplomacy. Artists seldom confined themselves to a single art, and writers wrote on a variety of subjects with a bold confidence that would be unthinkable in today's specialized world.

The universal man marked the height of the Renaissance concept of human potential. By the mid-16th century, a new ideal had formed, described by the writer and diplomat Baldassare Castiglione in *The Courtier.* On its deepest level, *The Courtier* is a thoughtful examination of humanist ideas, but it became popular throughout Europe as a bible for good manners and correct behavior. Like the universal man, Castiglione's courtier was expected to do many things well—but he was supposed to do them easily, lightly, "so as to conceal all art and make whatever is done and said appear to be without effort and without almost any thought about it." This ideal produced charming, cultured dilettantes who dabbled at all the arts but mastered none.

The progression of the male ideal—from public-minded businessman to multi-talented genius to charming courtly companion—is symbolic of the rise and fall of Renaissance culture and the growing despotism of Renaissance politics. From a thriving land of active citizens, Italy gradually became a culture of courtiers who maintained their place only by pleasing their all-powerful prince.

MARRIAGE AND FAMILY LIFE

Marriage and the family formed the backbone of Renaissance society. Although peasants in the countryside often lived with several generations under one roof, the most typical household in the towns was the nuclear family of a husband, wife, and children. In wealthier families, infants were turned over to wet nurses, who often cared for them in their own homes. But once children grew out of the nursing stage and returned home, they were generally treated with great affection.

Affection between husband and wife was a different matter. Renaissance marriages were not love matches; they were contracts arranged to strengthen a family's financial and social position. In order to arrange a good match, a woman had to have a substantial dowry that could test the financial resources of even the wealthiest families—and less attractive daughters were often urged to enter the religious life in order to save the expense of a dowry. Yet no matter how much money a wife brought into the marriage, her husband exercised complete control over the family's finances.

The typical Renaissance match was between a teenage girl and an older man, which made it even more difficult for a couple to connect on a personal level. Yet many married couples did develop a genuine love for each other. In 1445 a Florentine silk merchant named Luca da Panzano wrote touchingly of his wife in his diary:

> I record how Lucrezia my wife, by whom I have 11 children living, died on the day [November] 5 at half-past two in the night, on Friday evening; which pains me as much as if it had been myself, since she has been my companion 20 years, one month and ten days . . . this woman was a great loss, and all the people of Florence were hurt, because she was a good and sweet woman, and had a way of making herself loved by all who knew her.

Despite such warm sentiments, mistresses and illegitimate children were so common during the Renaissance that there was little stigma attached to illegitimate birth, and some of the greatest figures of the age were born outside of marriage: Francesco Sforza, Leon Battista Alberti, Leonardo da Vinci, Cesare and Lucrezia Borgia. In order to preserve their own social standing, wives were forced to ignore their husbands' extramarital affairs, while some women engaged in their own affairs. However, many cultured ladies apparently satisfied their romantic frustrations by heated conversation and correspondence with the charming courtiers who were drawn to them like moths to a flame.

Underneath the everyday reality of marriage as a social contract was a strange philosophical argument expressed in a famous saying of the Middle Ages: "No man can serve a wife and philosophy." The fourth-century Christian philosopher Saint Jerome had mistakenly attributed this saying to Cicero; but even after Coluccio Salutati discovered Cicero's letters and established that the great philosopher himself had been married twice, Renaissance humanists and churchmen took a dim view of married life. Salutati's protégé, Poggio Bracciolini, steadfastly refused to marry, though he had a dozen children by a mistress. At the same time, the fiery Christian preacher Saint Bernardino of Siena proclaimed, "I believe so few are saved among those in the married state that, of a thousand marriages, nine hundred and ninety-nine seem to be marriages of the Devil."

Gradually, however, this attitude changed. In the late 1430s, the humanist Leon Battista Alberti enthusiastically praised the virtues of married love in his treatise on the family. Even the old bachelor Poggio finally married and became an enthusiastic convert to the joys of marriage. In a society where a woman's status depended almost completely on her status in marriage, this more positive view of married life—along with the growing leisure of the wealthy class—provided greater freedom for women to develop their own human potential.

THE ROLE OF WOMEN

Renaissance society was almost completely dominated by men; they held the wealth and political power and played the active role in art and literature. The birth of sons was celebrated joyously, and an enlightened family like the Este of Ferrara might welcome their first daughter with almost as much joy as a son. But the birth of a second daughter caused no celebration at all, and in poorer families many baby

FESTIVALS AND MUSIC

The people of the Renaissance loved colorful festivals, sports, and celebrations. Carnival, which lasted from the day after Christmas until the beginning of Lent, was an almost continuous period of gay revelry, with parades, horse races, banquets, and mock battles. Men dressed as women, women dressed as men, and masked singers wandered through the streets serenading the citizens with bawdy songs. Naturally, it was the wealthy class who could afford to indulge their passion for fun and games, but the carnival parades and other public festivals throughout the year provided a welcome relief from the hard daily life of the working classes as well.

Each Italian city had a patron saint, whose special day was a cause not only for religious observance but for celebrating the greatness of the city itself. In Siena, whose patroness was the Virgin Mary, the feast of the Assumption was celebrated by a wild horse race through the streets and a huge procession in the public square, with citizens from different neighborhoods marching in costume behind trumpeters, banners, and rolling floats of animals—not that different from the floats in our parades today. Florence celebrated St. John's day in similar fashion, inspiring one spectator to write, "The whole city is given over to revelry and feasting . . . so that this whole earth seems like a paradise." Venice celebrated the Feast of the Ascension with an old tradition in which the doge sailed out on his official state barge and threw a ring into the Adriatic Sea, symbolizing the marriage of Venice and the sea.

The sounds of trumpets and strings and songs were a joyous part of everyday life. Trumpeters not only led official processions; they accompanied brides to the church, announced the passage of dignitaries through the streets, and even called attention to the arrival of food at fancy dinner parties. No Renaissance social gathering was complete without songs and music; artists, philosophers, and noble ladies all prided themselves on their musical accomplishments. Leonardo da Vinci first went to Milan to demonstrate a new stringed instrument

Colorful, varied entertainments were popular at Renaissance courts. In this mid-15th century panel painting from the workshop of Apollonio di Giovanni, an acrobat and wrestlers perform, with lute players strumming in the background. (Ashmolean Museum, Oxford)

he had invented, while Leon Battista Alberti praised his own talent in his autobiography: "He delighted in the organ and was considered an expert among the leading musicians."

Despite Alberti's boasts and the delight in social music, the Italian Renaissance was not an age of great musical composition on the level of the accomplishments in art and literature. During most of the period the leading composers were not native Italians, but rather visitors from France or Flanders, who brought new, richer concepts of harmony. However, these foreigners were clearly influenced by the secular spirit of the Italian Renaissance. Josquin des Prés, a great Flemish composer who worked for many years in Italy, used a popular nonreligious tune in writing music for the Mass. At the same time, both foreign and Italian composers helped bring "serious" music out of the Church, developing a multivoice song style called the madrigal and composing sophisticated musical entertainments for Renaissance courts.

The humanists were fascinated with music in a mathematical sense, and Franchino Gafori was an important teacher of music theory in late 15th-century Milan. However, it was not until the second half of the 16th century that Italy produced a great native composer. Working primarily in Rome, Giovanni Pierluigi da Palestrina established a new level of religious vocal music in his compositions for the Mass. He employed sophisticated harmony and melody while also carefully matching the music with the meaning of the words. By Palestrina's time, Renaissance culture had faded, but in the following centuries, Italy would become one of the most important centers of European music.

daughters were abandoned and left to die. It's hardly surprising that studies of population show a higher percentage of men than women in Renaissance Italy.

Some women found independence in the religious life, where they could rise to a position of power as head of a convent. Other women found a different sort of independence as high-class prostitutes called courtesans, who were famous throughout Europe for their learning as well as their beauty. But most women were destined for marriage, and married life was never an equal contract. Some upper-class women were well-educated, patronized the arts, and exercised substantial influence over the men in their lives; but they were still treated primarily as possessions—first of their fathers, then of their husbands. And in later life, even a brilliant woman like Isabella d'Este could exercise power only through her influence over her son.

Despite these limitations, women made important strides during the Renaissance, as feminine ideals evolved along with the ideals of men. During the 14th century, the attitude toward women was formed by two competing ideas from the Middle Ages. On the one hand, Christianity portrayed women as a source of sin and temptation, just as Eve had tempted Adam with the forbidden apple. On the other hand, the medieval French troubadours elevated women to a pedestal of unattainable perfection, on which men were supposed to love and worship them from afar. Dante and Petrarch both reflected this tradition, idealizing their love for women they could never have, while ignoring the real women in their lives.

This early Renaissance view of woman as either sinful temptress or idealized goddess left little room for human development. The Black Death may have been a turning point, however, since those who survived carried a new sense of strength and destiny, regardless of their gender. In the *Decameron,* Boccaccio begins with seven young ladies who want to escape the plague-infested city—a daring plan hardly in keeping with previous views of women. But then he backs off from this boldness, and the women decide they can't go without the company of men. "Men are a woman's head," says one of the women, "and we can rarely succeed in anything without their help." Despite this, Boccaccio portrays the women realistically and intelligently, and the stories they tell are as funny and bawdy as the stories told by the men.

Real change began in the 15th century, demonstrated in two generations of the Medici family. In 1414 Cosimo de' Medici married Contessina Bardi, the daughter of an old, wealthy Florentine family who had all the advantages available to women of her time. Though she could read and write, she knew nothing of classical studies and confined her efforts to being a thrifty housekeeper and keeping her family well-fed. However, her daughter-in-law, Lucrezia Tornabuoni, wife of Piero de' Medici and mother of Lorenzo, wrote classical poetry, miracle plays, and religious songs. When she suffered from lower back pain, she not only soaked in therapeutic waters herself, she bought the land around the baths and built a large brick bathhouse for the people of Florence.

The next two generations brought even greater emancipation. Caterina Sforza, daughter of the ill-fated Duke Galeazzo Maria Sforza of Milan, had little interest in culture, but she pursued love and politics with a bold ruthlessness that left a trail of broken hearts and dead bodies. Isabella and Beatrice d'Este, Elizabetta Gonzaga, and Lucrezia Borgia all played leading roles in the culture of their husbands' courts, while Isabella and Lucrezia also exercised substantial political power while their husbands were away. (For more on the d'Este sisters and

These sketches by Antonio Pisanello depict the extreme style of men's clothing and the plucked forehead for women that became fashionable during the 1430s. (Ashmolean Museum, Oxford)

Lucrezia Borgia, see the box features of Chapter 6 and Chapter 4 respectively.) At the end of the 15th century, Alessandra Scala, daughter of the Florentine chancellor, attended classes at the University of Florence and became so proficient in Greek that she could recite the entire tragedy of *Electra* in the original.

Although these women were unusual, they reflected a new freedom, especially in Florence and other enlightened cities. According to historian Vincent Cronin, "the average well-to-do Florentine woman of the fifteenth century certainly received a better education and enjoyed a fuller life than her predecessors. She walked out more often, attended dances, had an opportunity of showing off her beauty and accomplishments."

The pursuit of beauty was a full-time occupation for some Renaissance women. Dark-haired Italian ladies spent hours bleaching their hair in the sun to achieve the ideal blonde look, and many women plucked their hair to create a fashionable high forehead. From the old concepts of simplicity, styles of clothing became extreme for both men and women. Men wore colorful form-fitting tights and short doublets, while women wore low-cut, gold-brocaded gowns and platform shoes so high that the wearers had to be supported by their maids when walking in the street. Many cities passed laws against excessively ornate clothing, but fashionable people wore it anyway.

Women like Lucrezia Tornabuoni and Isabella d'Este wrote poetry and witty correspondence, and Isabella was confident enough to make a sketch for a work of art that she commissioned. But it wasn't until the mid-16th century, after the height of the Renaissance had passed, that women took their place among the active writers and artists. The most famous female poet was Vittoria Colonna, a Roman noblewoman who was admired by Michelangelo. But the best and most original poetess was a middle-class Venetian named Gaspara Stampa, who died around the age of 30 in 1554, leaving behind 218 sonnets portraying her desperate, unhappy love affair with a nobleman. Although Stampa idealized her lover in the style of Petrarch, she described every emotional high and low with a fresh honesty that moved beyond the academic tone of humanist writing:

> I burned, I wept, I sang; I burn, sing, weep again,
> And I shall weep and sing, I shall forever burn
> Until dark death or time or fortune's turn
> Shall still my eye and heart, still fire and pain.

The finest female artist of the Renaissance was Sofonisba Anguissola, a noblewoman born in the town of Cremona in 1532, who studied painting with the aging Michelangelo. In the years after Italy was conquered by Spain, Anguissola was invited to the court of King Philip II in Madrid. It's typical of the attitude toward women that—though her artistic talent earned her the invitation—her official position was lady-in-waiting to the queen, rather than court painter. However, during almost 20 years in Spain, Anguissola formed an important connection between the painting style of the Italian Renaissance and the court painting of the Spanish Renaissance.

Gaspara Stampa and Sofonisba Anguissola lived at the tail end of the Italian Renaissance, and their independent lives were not representative of the age. So it would be a mistake to see this period as a time of freedom for women in the modern sense of the word. Yet, for some extraordinary women, the Renaissance offered new opportunity for development and self-expression. While royal ladies like Isabella d'Este commanded respect for their political and cultural insight, Stampa and Anguissola emerged as poets and artists in their own right, giving new voice to women in a changing world.

CHAPTER 10 NOTES

p. 103   "so as to conceal . . ." Baldassare Castiglione. *The Courtier;* quoted in *Horizon Book*, p. 317.

p. 104   "I record how Lucrezia . . ." Luca da Panzano; quoted in John Gage. *Life in Italy at the Time of the Medici* (New York: Capricorn Books, 1968), pp. 182-83.

p. 105   "I believe so few are saved . . ." Saint Bernardino of Siena; quoted in Vincent Cronin, *The Florentine Renaissance*, p. 79.

p. 106   "The whole city . . ." Anonymous observer; quoted in Hale. *Renaissance*, p. 150.

p. 107   "He delighted in the organ . . ." Leon Battista Alberti; quoted in *Horizon Book*, p. 331.

p. 109   "Men are a woman's head . . ." Boccaccio; quoted in Aldington, trans. p. 39.

p. 110   "the average well-to-do Florentine woman . . ." Cronin, *The Florentine Renaissance*, p. 84.

p. 111   "I burned, I wept . . ." Gaspara Stampa, *Rime;* quoted in Cronin. *Flowering of the Renaissance*, p. 187.

THE FOREIGN INVASIONS:

End of an Era

Strange as it may seem, the Italian Renaissance did not actually occur in *Italy,* and the great scholars, artists, and rulers were not really *Italians.* We use these words today, but the people of the Renaissance viewed their world more locally. First and foremost, they were loyal to their families; they were Medicis or Borgias or Gonzagas. Beyond family, there was the city-state and perhaps the region. The citizens of Florence were Florentines or Tuscans, not Italians; and the citizens of other city-states had similar feelings. Most educated people understood the Italian language—although some called it Tuscan—and cultural ideas passed from city to city. But there was no sense of an Italian nation.

The variety and independence of the Italian city-states contributed greatly to the richness of Renaissance culture. But while the city-states developed their economy, their arts, and their own unique brand of diplomacy and politics, other Europeans developed a larger and more powerful political structure: not the city-state, but the nation-state. Of course, the Italians were aware of what was happening elsewhere in

Europe, but the city-states were too busy worrying about each other to see that the greatest danger lay outside the Italian peninsula.

The wealth of Europe began to shift as well. The fall of Constantinople to the Turks in 1453 cut into the lucrative eastern Mediterranean trade, while the "discovery" of the New World in 1492 by Christopher Columbus brought new riches to the nations that faced the Atlantic Ocean. Ironically, Columbus was from Genoa, and his voyage was financed by Venetian bankers—but the rulers who borrowed the money were Ferdinand and Isabella of Spain. It was the Spanish flag that Columbus planted in the sands of the New World, and it was the Spanish treasury that grew rich from American silver. In the end it was Spain that would rule Italy. But first came the French.

THE INVASION OF 1494

Charles VIII became King of France at the age of 13. Like many young men, he dreamed of doing something wonderful and chivalrous in the traditions of medieval knights. Of course, Charles had more power than most young men, and his dreams were grand: He wanted to reestablish the French claims to Naples and set off on a Crusade against the Turks in the eastern Mediterranean. It wasn't a logical plan; France had more important interests in northern Europe. But it was the young king's dream.

Lodovico Sforza also had a dream: he wanted to rule Milan as the rightful duke. He already dominated the city-state and ruled in the style of the wealthiest Renaissance princes. But his nephew, Gian Galeazzo, held the title of duke, and though he had no personal interest in ruling, his wife was not happy with her inferior position. To a man of Lodovico's ruthlessness and cunning, this would have been a simple matter of killing his nephew—except that his nephew's wife, Isabella of Aragon, happened to be the granddaughter of the king of Naples, one of the most powerful forces in Italy. So Lodovico encouraged Charles VIII, now in his early twenties, to follow his dream and take care of his problem in Naples.

In September 1494, Charles entered Italy at the head of the mightiest army ever seen on the Italian peninsula—some 30,000 soldiers carrying new, heavy artillery. They passed through Lodovico's Milan and moved on to Florence, where Piero de' Medici, son of Lorenzo the Magnificent, made a less than magnificent attempt at diplomacy that

This imaginative sketch by Leonardo da Vinci depicts a foundry for building giant cannon, but the foreign invaders were more advanced in the practical use of field artillery. (Original in the Royal Library, Windsor; photo courtesy Rare Books Division, Library of Congress)

resulted in the French army parading through the streets while Piero was driven into exile. The French continued south toward Rome, where Pope Alexander VI also failed to resist them, and finally marched triumphantly into Naples in February 1495.

By this time, Lodovico realized that he had made a big mistake. His nephew died shortly after the invasion—possibly by poison—and Lodovico was finally the duke of Milan. Now the greatest threat to his power was Charles himself, who had claims on Milan through an old marriage between the French royal family and the Visconti. King Ferdinand of Spain, whose family had ruled Naples, wasn't too happy about the situation either. At Ferdinand's urging, Milan, Venice, and Pope Alexander VI joined with Spain and the Holy Roman Empire in an anti-French alliance called the League of Venice. When the league mustered a large army in Milanese territory, Charles left half his army in Naples and marched north to meet them at Fornovo in July 1495. Although both sides claimed victory, the French sustained fewer casualties and marched back to France.

On the surface, Charles's expedition seems like no more than a strange interlude in the Italian Renaissance. He marched into Italy and marched out again a year later, leaving soldiers in Naples—and within another year his garrisons had been driven out by supporters of the Aragons. Yet, to the 16th-century Italian historian Francesco Guicciardini—and to most of his contemporaries—1494 was the great turning point, "a most unhappy year for Italy, and in truth the beginning of those years of misfortune, because it opened the door to innumerable horrible calamities." The calamities included renewed local conflict, most notably in Florence, where pro-French republicans fought for years with the anti-French Medici faction. But the most horrible of the calamities was the series of invasions from the north. To put it simply, Charles VIII showed the rest of Europe that Italy was there for the taking.

THE WARS OF ITALY

The long series of wars that followed the invasion of 1494 are so complex and by modern standards so downright bizarre—that the 20th-century historian John R. Hale pointed out, "Since Guicciardini's *History of Italy* no historian has had the stomach to deal fully with them." We don't have the stomach, either. But a quick summary sheds fascinating light on the constantly shifting, personal politics of Europe in the 16th century.

Charles died in 1498, while planning to return to Italy and retake Naples. His successor, Louis XII, invaded northern Italy in 1499, drove out Lodovico Sforza, and established French control of Milan. The following year, Louis and King Ferdinand of Spain agreed to invade Naples together and share the kingdom between them. Not surprisingly, the alliance soon collapsed, and in December 1503 the Spanish army soundly defeated the French, gaining control of southern Italy and establishing a bloody pattern of Spanish-French battles on Italian soil.

The only major Italian power left untouched by the early invasions was Venice, whose land empire lay in the northeast, out of the invaders' path. In late 1508 and early 1509 an amazing assortment of old foes forgot their differences and banded together in the anti-Venetian League of Cambrai: Louis of France, Ferdinand of Spain, the Holy Roman Emperor Maximilian, Pope Julius II, the Gonzaga of Mantua, and the Este of Ferrara. At first, the League was successful, and the French army handed Venice a decisive defeat at Agnadello. But in a flash of delayed inspiration, Julius realized that the complete defeat of Venice would leave the Papal States hemmed in by foreign powers. In classic Italian style, he made peace with Venice and brought it into a new anti-French alliance with Spain, the Holy Roman Empire, Switzerland, and England.

Pope Julius himself led his armies in several battles and introduced a new battle cry: "Out with the barbarians!" Faced with the combined forces, the French "barbarians" withdrew from Italy in 1512, and Lodovico Sforza's son was restored to rule in Milan, while Medici rule was restored to Florence. For a few short years, northern and central Italy was again in the hands of Italians. It wouldn't last. The barbarians—French and otherwise—would be back.

In January 1515, 20-year-old Francis I became king of France and immediately prepared to invade Italy. That September, Francis led his forces against the Swiss near Milan in a two-day battle that marked a turning point in European warfare. Until then, the well-disciplined Swiss infantrymen had set the standard of military strategy by attacking in a solid mass with long, sharp pikes stretched out to kill anyone standing in their way. But the French employed horse-drawn artillery so effectively that the Swiss left over 10,000 dead on the field of battle and retreated to the border they still share with Italy today. Francis went on to establish control over most of the northwest, including Milan and Genoa. It was the height of French power in Italy—but a new and even more powerful ruler was already emerging to take it away.

Charles V was born in the year 1500, the grandson of King Ferdinand and Queen Isabella of Spain on one side and of the Holy Roman Emperor Maximilian on the other side. At the age of six, he inherited his father's holdings in the Netherlands, but that was only the beginning. In 1516, when Ferdinand died, Charles became king of Spain, inheriting not only Spain itself but its colonies in the New World and its Italian territories in Naples and Sicily. When Maximilian died three years later, 19-year-old Charles inherited the Habsburg family lands in Germany and Austria and was elected Holy Roman Emperor. For the first time since the Middle Ages, here was an emperor who actually had an empire.

Francis I happened to be Charles's cousin, and the young emperor put the situation succinctly in 1521, saying, "My cousin Francis and I are in perfect accord; he wants Milan and so do I." Charles and Francis waged a series of conflicts over Milan, culminating in the battle of Pavia in February 1525, where the French were routed by imperial troops and Francis was taken prisoner. "All is lost save honor," he wrote to his mother, "—and my skin, which is safe." Francis's skin remained safely under Charles's control for 11 months, until he finally agreed to a long series of demands, which included giving up all his claims to Italy.

As soon as he returned to France, Francis announced that he had no intention of honoring promises made under the pressure of imprisonment, and Pope Clement VII—who was a Medici—graciously absolved him from his oaths. Francis and the pope then formed yet another league that planned to divide Italy among various Italian and French powers and challenged the emperor to agree to their new arrangement or face war. Charles was a staunch Catholic who had supported the Medici in Florence and the pope in Rome. But when he failed to win Clement over through diplomacy, he sent a combined force of over 20,000 German and Spanish mercenaries against the Holy City.

On May 6, 1527, while Clement and his advisors took refuge in the fortress of Castel Sant' Angelo, the army swarmed over the city walls and began eight days of wild destruction. They demanded ransom money from every citizen, killing those who didn't pay and some who did. They destroyed books and precious works of art, and took special delight in torturing cardinals and other churchmen. They assaulted women so ferociously that many young Roman women drowned themselves in the Tiber River rather than face rape at the hands of the barbarians. When it was over, perhaps 10,000 Romans were dead, thousands more had fled, and the damage to the city ran into what would be hundreds of millions of dollars today. The damage to Italian pride was greater. Even the Dutch humanist Erasmus recognized the sense of loss: "Rome was not alone the shrine of the Christian faith, the nurse of noble souls, and the abode of the Muses, but the mother of nations. To how many was she not dearer and sweeter and more precious than their own land! . . . In truth this is not the ruin of one city, but of the whole world."

Back in Spain, Charles was not happy with the destruction by his soldiers. But he pressed his advantage with the pope and out-maneuvered Francis with help from the Genoese admiral Andrea Doria. In 1529 the French formally renounced their Italian claims, and Charles traveled triumphantly to Bologna—the first time he had ever visited Italy. There, on February 24, 1530, a badly beaten Clement formally crowned him as the Holy Roman Emperor, the last emperor ever crowned by a pope. Italy had come full circle. The Renaissance had arisen when the emperor left the city-states to develop along their own path. Now the emperor was back, and—politically at least—the age of the Renaissance was over.

Sporadic fighting between France and the Empire continued for 30 years, but another treaty in 1559 firmly sealed Spanish control of Italy. Charles had died the previous year; but even before his death he'd grown weary of trying to rule the world and had divided his empire, giving Spain and Italy to his son, Philip II. Until the early 18th century, Spain ruled Milan, Naples, and Sicily directly while controlling puppet states in Genoa and Florence and exercising substantial influence over the papacy. Of the great Italian powers, only Venice retained its independence.

THE COUNTER-REFORMATION AND CULTURAL DECLINE

The foreign invasions didn't end Renaissance culture immediately, except perhaps in Florence, where the original invasion of Charles VIII led directly to the anticultural rule of the religious zealot Savonarola. The Renaissance in Milan continued for a few more years, until Lodovico Sforza was driven out in 1499. But Rome actually reached the height of its Renaissance in the midst of the invasions, and even after the sack of the city in 1527, work continued on St. Peter's, and Michelangelo painted his great fresco of *The Last Judgment* on the wall of the Sistine Chapel. In Venice, Renaissance culture continued well into the second half of the 16th century.

So it would be overly simplistic to say that the Italian Renaissance ended because of the invasions. However, the foreign armies brought a new, bloodier level of warfare that decimated the population in northern Italy and deeply disturbed the psyche of the Italian people. In fact, some historians see the exaggerated, disjointed style of Mannerist art as a direct reflection of the chaotic and violent political situation during the later invasions. And Spain's ultimate domination of the peninsula brought a new cultural perspective that made Italy less "Italian." But there were other factors as well, and the most significant was a new attitude within the Catholic Church.

The Church during the Renaissance was incredibly corrupt, but it was surprisingly tolerant of free expression. To some extent this tolerance was a direct result of the corruption; Renaissance popes and cardinals had so many skeletons in their own closets that they weren't in a position to pass strict moral judgments on others. But it was also the spirit of the age—an attitude that human beings had the right to follow the path of their own thoughts and inspiration, as long as they stayed within the larger framework of Christianity. Occasionally, progressive thinkers like Lorenzo Valla and Pico della Mirandola ran afoul of the papacy, but they weren't killed for their ideas.

That changed in the mid-16th century, when the Catholic Church began a major reform movement in response to the Protestant Reformation that was sweeping through northern Europe. The Church movement, called the Counter-Reformation or Catholic Reformation, involved much-needed reform of Church doctrine and the clergy, but it also included new efforts to control individual thoughts and beliefs. The Spaniards had led the way by reestablishing a medieval institution called the Inquisition in 1480. Charged with finding and punishing heretics, the Spanish Inquisitors went about their task with ruthless enthusiasm, using a variety of ingenious tortures to obtain confessions from those suspected of thinking wrong thoughts.

In 1542, as the Spanish solidified their hold on Italy, Pope Paul III established the Inquisition in Rome. Paul also gave formal approval to the Spanish Jesuits, the most fanatical of Church reformers, and he called the Council of Trent, a meeting of Church leaders that affirmed many reforms as Church law. In other ways, however, Paul was still a Renaissance pope. Born into a wealthy family and educated in the humanist tradition, he built beautiful palaces, made his grandsons cardinals, and patronized Michelangelo. But more fanatical popes followed, particularly Paul IV, who increased the activity of the Inquisition and published the first "Index of Prohibited Books" in 1559.

The new attitude of the Church led to the persecution of Italian intellectuals, including the philosopher Giordano Bruno, who was burned at the stake in the year 1600, and the great scientist Galileo Galilei, who was forced in 1633 to publicly renounce his belief that the Earth revolved around the sun. A century earlier, Copernicus's ideas of a sun-centered system had been explained to Pope Clement VII without causing serious objection; even in the waning days of the Renaissance, such ideas were deemed worthy of consideration. But under the harsh rule of the Inquisition, only approved ideas could be considered. The free spirit of the Renaissance was dead.

CHAPTER 11 NOTES

p. 116   "a most unhappy year . . ." Francesco Guicciardini. *The History of Italy*, trans. and ed. Sidney Alexander (New York: Macmillan, 1969), p. 32.

p. 116   "Since Guicciardini's *History* . . ." Hale. p. 142.

p. 118   "My cousin Francis . . ." Charles V; quoted in Durant. p. 621.

p. 118   "All is lost . . ." Francis I; quoted in Durant. p.626.

p. 119   "Rome was not . . ." Desiderius Erasmus; quoted in Durant. p. 633.

EUROPE AND THE MODERN WORLD:

Legacy of the Italian Renaissance

Italy is separated from the rest of Europe by the Alps in the north and the sea everywhere else. But the mountains and the sea can both be crossed, and from the earliest days of the Renaissance, Italian ideas circulated in northern and western Europe.

The largest force of cultural ambassadors were the Italian bankers, traders, and diplomats who played such an important role in the financial and political affairs of Europe. But scholars and artists traveled as well. Petrarch carried his early brand of humanism with him in his travels through France and Switzerland, while the English writer Geoffrey Chaucer visited Italy twice in the 1370s, where he discovered the works of Dante, Petrarch, and Boccaccio. Half a century later, the humanist poet Aeneas Silvius (later Pope Pius II) traveled widely throughout Europe and served the Holy Roman Emperor in Germany, where he was known as "the apostle of humanism." At the same time, the papal administration in Rome and the famed Italian universities at

Padua and Bologna brought scholars from other European countries to Italy. The French painter Jean Fouquet visited Rome before 1450 and returned to France with a new understanding of perspective.

The development of the printing press during the second half of the 15th century was a major turning point in the spread of ideas, as classical works and Italian writings circulated on a wider level than ever possible before. Printed books also helped spread Italian art, not only through dissertations on painting, sculpture, and architecture, but through books of engravings that hinted at the wonders awaiting in Italy.

Ironically, the foreign invasions—which ultimately destroyed the Renaissance in Italy—played an important role in spreading Renaissance culture. When King Louis XII of France invaded Milan, he was so impressed by Leonardo's fresco of *The Last Supper* that he wanted to cut it down from the wall and take it back with him to France. Instead, he brought a number of minor Italian artists to his court, and his successor, Francis I, brought Leonardo himself to France, where he died in 1519. According to one story, the young French king held the aged Italian genius in his arms as he died. Whether or not this was true on a real level, it was definitely true on a symbolic level. For by the early 16th century, the rest of Europe had begun to firmly embrace the culture of the Italian Renaissance.

THE FLEMISH RENAISSANCE, GERMANY, AND NORTHERN HUMANISM

In the early 15th century, as the Florentine Renaissance blossomed with the youthful vigor of Brunelleschi, Donatello, and Masaccio, another artistic Renaissance was underway in Flanders, a region of the Netherlands. Usually called the Flemish Renaissance, it was not a complete cultural movement like the Italian Renaissance, and it didn't have the strong philosophical base of classical studies and humanism. However, it grew out of a social and economic structure similar to that found in Italy: the glittering court of the duke of Burgundy, large town populations with a wealthy merchant class to support the court, and a thriving class of creative artisans.

The Flemish Renaissance was marked by careful realism and strong colors in painting and by new developments of harmony in music.

Flemish painters and composers traveled to Italy, where the artists introduced techniques of oil painting while the composers dominated the Italian musical scene. At the same time, the Flemish were influenced by Italian ideas, particularly the elegant simplicity of Italian paintings and the Italian love of vocal music. A century later, Michelangelo scoffed at Flemish painting, writing, "They paint in Flanders only to deceive the external eye." But the realistic style of Flanders influenced European art, particularly in Germany and France, before Italian art became widely known.

The first renaissance outside Italy and Flanders began in Germany in the late 15th century. There again, the situation was similar to that in Italy, with a variety of wealthy and semi-independent towns. The most important artistic figure was the painter and engraver Albrecht Dürer, who was influenced by both Flemish art, which he could see in northern Europe, and Italian art—which he first observed in books of rough engravings that circulated in Germany. In 1494 Dürer traveled to Venice to see the original paintings, and, like many European artists who followed him, became mystically obsessed with Italy and Italian art:

> He believed that the formula for successful painting of the human figure, like some ancient mystery, was kept hidden by Italian artists. He sought the magic formula in Italy itself, deepened his imagination, improved his technique, but never found what he sought, and to his death the Gothic tradition into which he had been born held him in thrall. Yet without his Italian experiences and without his preoccupation with Italian art, his own achievements would have been less noble.

Like Leonardo da Vinci, Dürer was not only an artist, but a student of anatomy, botany, mathematics, zoology, and engineering. In truth, he was an *uomo universale*—perhaps the first universal man north of the Alps.

Dürer's friend and contemporary, the humanist Desiderius Erasmus, was also a Renaissance man, though he confined his efforts to writing and scholarship. Erasmus is considered by many historians to be the greatest of all the humanists, more insightful and original than the Italians who came before him. A native of Rotterdam in the Netherlands, Erasmus corresponded with scholars throughout Europe, lectured at Cambridge in England, worked in the library of Bologna, and played a central role in the German Renaissance. Taking full advantage of the printing press, Erasmus became the first writer in history to make a living strictly from the sale of his books.

Like most northern humanists, Erasmus was more concerned with religious and spiritual questions than were the Italian humanists. He wrote a scathing satire of the corruption in the Church, edited the first printed version of the New Testament in the original Greek, and then created a new, purer Latin translation based on the Greek text—hoping to end theological conflict and bring Christians closer to the true meaning of Christ's life and words. Although he was a friend of Martin Luther and shared many of Luther's concerns, he refused to break from the Church. Dürer, on the other hand, firmly supported Luther, and tried to convince Erasmus to join them. For all its high-minded idealism, the Protestant Reformation that Luther started in 1517 was essentially a puritanical movement that ended the free spirit of Renaissance thought and art in Germany.

Erasmus was also friends with the English humanist Sir Thomas More, who shared his staunch Catholicism and his concern with spiritual ideas. Unlike Erasmus, who died in bed, More paid for his beliefs with his head when he refused to support King Henry VIII's divorce. More's most famous work, *Utopia*, is a portrait of an ideal society that draws on both his observations of contemporary politics and his readings of Plato. The French humanist Guillaume Budé followed more directly in the secular footsteps of the Italians, using close textual scholarship to demonstrate how language and legal texts change over the centuries.

Dürer, Erasmus, More, and Budé were of the same generation; they were all born between 1466 and 1478 and died between 1528 and 1540. Thus, there was a thriving humanist movement in northern Europe by the year 1500, and in Germany, there was an artistic Renaissance led by Dürer and continuing with other German artists like Hans Holbein the Younger. Art also continued to develop in the Netherlands, where Hieronymus Bosch created wildly original and colorful fantasies that depicted the underlying human condition behind the facade of realism.

The German Renaissance meets the English Renaissance in this 1527 portrait of English humanist Sir Thomas More by German artist Hans Holbein the Younger, who came to England as official court painter for King Henry VIII. (Copyright The Frick Collection, New York)

THE RENAISSANCE IN FRANCE, ENGLAND, AND SPAIN

While France conquered Italy with cannons and soldiers, Italy conquered France with art and ideas. The Italian cultural invasion began in the last few years of the 15th century, when Charles VIII and Louis XII returned to France from their expeditions in Italy. But the French

Renaissance flowered under Francis I (reigned 1515–47), who turned the pursuit of culture into a national program. He brought Italian artists like Leonardo and Benvenuto Cellini to France, promising Cellini, "I will choke you with gold." Of course, a national renaissance cannot depend on foreigners, and Francis also sponsored the efforts of French artists and architects to develop their own style, combining Italian and French ideas.

Just as the Italian Renaissance had led to the development of the Italian language, so the French Renaissance led to new literary respect for the French language. French poets and musicians created a poetic song form called the *chanson,* while Francis's sister Marguerite de Navarre wrote bawdy stories and spiritual poems. Even bawdier was the French monk Rabelais, whose satirical tales of two giants, *Gargantua and Pantagruel,* are among the greatest masterpieces of Renaissance literature.

In England, the Renaissance blossomed during the reign of Elizabeth I (1558–1603), who presided over a cultured court that was distinguished in many areas, including politics, manners, and music. However, the greatest achievements were in literature, where English writers began by imitating the sonnets of Petrarch and the stories of Boccaccio but soon developed their own distinctive style—creating an explosion of brilliance in the English language that continued long after Elizabeth's death. From 1580 to 1680, England produced a group of poets and playwrights that is unequaled in any similar period of time in any other nation. As a period of pure artistic genius, English Renaissance literature is comparable only to Italian Renaissance art.

This is the age of Edmund Spenser's narrative fantasy *The Faerie Queen,* John Milton's brilliant epic *Paradise Lost,* and the strikingly modern metaphysical poetry of John Donne and Andrew Marvell. In Elizabethan drama, Christopher Marlowe and Ben Jonson would be considered among the world's greatest playwrights, had they not been overshadowed by the astonishing brilliance and artistic production of William Shakespeare. Ironically, Shakespeare made fun of his countrymen's efforts to copy Italian styles of dress and behavior, while basing many of his plays on Italian stories. For the English, Italy was both a real source of inspiration and a less real land of dark doings and deadly intrigue. By setting social and political problems in far-off Italy,

English writers could more safely examine the dangerous situation in their own land.

The development of a native Spanish Renaissance came even later than the Renaissance in England. When Charles V conquered Italy in the early 16th century, he was just as impressed with Italian art as his rival Francis I had been. Charles decorated his huge palace in Madrid with paintings by the Venetian artists Titian and Tintoretto, and he had so much respect for their work that he once stopped to pick up a brush Titian had dropped. But when his successor Philip II (reigned 1556–98) asked Spanish artists to produce new works to hang beside the Italian masters, there was little creative response. It is perhaps a measure of his frustration with the native talent that Philip took the unusual step of bringing the female Italian painter Sofonisba Anguissola to his court.

There was one great Spanish painter of the later 16th century, but Philip didn't like his work. He's called El Greco, because he had originally come from the Greek island of Crete, but he studied in Italy and went on to work in Spain. El Greco developed the Mannerist style of elongated figures to a new level of dark, emotional intensity, and he is justly considered among the great painters of the world. The next great Spanish painter was Diego Velázquez, who lived half a century later and found far more favor with the Spanish court. The golden age of Spanish literature began in the early 17th century, with the novel *Don Quixote* by Miguel de Cervantes and the plays of Lope de Vega and Pedro Calderón. By this time, Italy was firmly under Spanish control, and the Italian Renaissance was rapidly fading into the past.

THE RENAISSANCE IN THE MODERN WORLD

The legacy of the Italian Renaissance has left an indelible mark on the culture of the modern world. The concepts of proper behavior detailed in Castiglione's *The Courtier* and other Italian books set the standard for the upper-class European lifestyle for hundreds of years. The English became obsessed with Italian culture, and a "Grand Tour" of Italy was an essential aspect of an English gentleman's education well into the 20th century. "A man who has not been in Italy," explained the English scholar Samuel Johnson, "is always conscious of an inferiority."

In America, the Founding Fathers were strongly influenced by Greek and Roman democracy, and Classical studies formed the backbone of early American education. Today, however, most Americans are more familiar with the English Renaissance, which blossomed almost a century after the height of the Renaissance in Italy. We enjoy the festive world of Elizabethan England at Renaissance fairs, and a recent film called *Renaissance Man* portrays a teacher who inspires young Army recruits with the genius of William Shakespeare. But in one powerful scene, the teacher—played by Danny DeVito—tells a student about Leon Battista Alberti. After listing Alberti's accomplishments in the arts, the teacher says, "But you know what I remember most about him? They say that he could stand with his feet together . . . and spring straight over a man's head." The student—an ex-football player—thinks about it for a while and replies, "So he was sort of like a smart jock then, right?" Alberti would have understood, although he never thought he was "sort of" anything.

In his *Notebooks*, Leonardo da Vinci expresses many ideas that were characteristic of the Renaissance and many others that reflected his own personal genius. But two simple statements stand out and express the spirit of the age: "The natural desire of good men is knowledge," and "Thou, O God, dost sell unto us all things at the price of labor." In the end this is the truest and greatest legacy of the Italian Renaissance:

We must seek to know, and we can do anything if we try.

CHAPTER 12 NOTES

p. 124   "They paint in Flanders . . ." Michelangelo; excerpted in Robert J. Clemens, ed. *Michelangelo: A Self-Portrait,* (Englewood Cliffs, NJ: Prentice-Hall, 1963), p. 37.

p. 124   "He believed that the formula . . ." J. H. Plumb, *Horizon Book*, p. 387.

p. 127   "I will choke you . . ." Francis I; quoted in *Horizon Book*, p. 393.

p. 128   "A man who . . ." Samuel Johnson; quoted in *Horizon Book*, p. 414.

p. 129   "The natural desire . . ." and "Thou, O God . . ." Leonardo da Vinci, *Notebooks;* excerpted in Gundersheimer. pp. 165, 176.

CHRONOLOGY

1250 • Holy Roman Emperor Frederick II dies.

c. 1300 • Early humanism develops in Padua and Verona.

1305 • Pope Clement V is crowned in Lyons; exile of papacy begins.

c. 1306 • Giotto completes frescoes in the Arena Chapel at Padua.

1309 • Avignon becomes official papal seat.

1321 • Dante completes *The Divine Comedy*.

1341 • Petrarch crowned poet laureate in Rome.

1347 • Cola di Rienzo proclaimed tribune in Rome.

1348–49 • Black Death ravages Italy.

1353 • Boccaccio completes the *Decameron*.

1377 • Pope Gregory IX returns to Rome.

1378 • Great Schism begins.

1380 • Venice defeats Genoa for supremacy of the sea.

1392 • Coluccio Salutati discovers Cicero's *Familiar Letters*.

1397 • Manuel Chrysolorus teaches Greek literature in Florence; Medici bank founded.

1401 • Lorenzo Ghiberti wins competition to design Baptistery doors.

1402 • Gian Galeazzo Visconti dies while planning attack on Florence.

c. 1403 • Brunelleschi and Donatello leave Florence for Rome.

1417 • Great Schism ends; Martin V becomes pope.

1423 • Vittorino da Feltre establishes humanist school in Mantua.

1427 • Masaccio paints his masterpiece, *The Tribute Money*.

1434 • Cosimo de' Medici rises to power in Florence.

1436 • Brunelleschi completes dome of Florence cathedral; Alberti writes treatise in Italian on painting.

1440 • Lorenzo Valla proves *Donation of Constantine* a forgery.

1440–42 • Donatello completes statue of *David*.

1443 • Alfonso of Aragon takes control of Naples.

1447 • The humanist Nicholas V becomes pope.

1450 • Francesco Sforza becomes ruler of Milan.

1453 • Constantinople falls to the Turks; Greek scholars flee to Italy.

1454–55 • Peace of Lodi begins.

1462 • Marsilio Ficino establishes Platonic Academy under patronage of Cosimo de' Medici.

1469 • Lorenzo de' Medici becomes ruler of Florence.

1471 • Sixtus IV becomes pope; begins strengthening Papal States.

1478–1480 • Pazzi Conspiracy, followed by war between Florence, Venice, Milan against the papacy, Naples, and Siena.

1480 • Lodovico Sforza seizes power in Milan.

1486 • Pico della Mirandola publishes his 900 theses and writes *Oration on the Dignity of Man*.

1490 • Isabella d'Este becomes marquise of Mantua.

1492 •	Lorenzo de' Medici dies; Columbus sails to New World.
1494 •	Charles VIII of France invades Italy; Medici expelled from Florence; German artist Albrecht Dürer visits Venice.
1498 •	Savonarola burned at the stake in Florence; Leonardo da Vinci completes *The Last Supper* in Milan.
1499 •	Louis XII of France invades Italy and conquers Milan.
1499–1503 •	Cesare Borgia conquers *Romagna* region of Papal States.
1503 •	Julius II becomes pope, bringing a new level of art patronage to Rome.
c. 1503–05 •	Leonardo paints the *Mona Lisa*.
1504 •	Michelangelo completes his statue of *David*.
1506 •	Donato Bramante designs St. Peter's basilica.
1508–09 •	League of Cambrai formed against Venice.
1508–12 •	Michelangelo paints the ceiling of the Sistine Chapel.
1508–1514 •	Raphael paints his frescoes in the Vatican.
1513 •	Giovanni de' Medici becomes Pope Leo X; Machiavelli writes *The Prince* (published 1532).
1515 •	Francis I becomes king of France and invades Italy.
1519 •	Charles V becomes Holy Roman Emperor.
1527 •	Rome is sacked by imperial troops.
1528 •	*The Courtier* by Baldassare Castiglione is published.
1530 •	Charles V crowned by Pope Clement VII in Bologna.
1541 •	Michelangelo completes *The Last Judgment* in the Sistine Chapel.
1542 •	Pope Paul III establishes Inquisition in Rome.
1543 •	Vesalius publishes book on anatomy; Copernicus publishes book on the solar system.

1559 • France formally renounces all claims to Italy; Spanish domination complete.

1564 • Michelangelo dies.

1576 • Titian dies.

FURTHER READING

Unless indicated otherwise, the following books are written for adults but should be clear and straightforward enough for young adult readers.

GENERAL HISTORIES

Cronin, Vincent. *The Florentine Renaissance* (New York: E. P. Dutton, 1967). An engaging, readable history of Florence during the 15th century, including fascinating personal details and anecdotes. Cronin accepts some reports that other scholars doubt, but overall this is one of the best books available to give the modern reader a sense of what the Renaissance was all about on the level of personal thought and artistic expression.

————. *The Flowering of the Renaissance* (New York: E. P. Dutton, 1969). A history of the Renaissance in Rome and Venice told in a similar readable and anecdotal style.

Duby, Georges, ed. *A History of Private Life, Vol. II: Revelations of the Medieval World*, Arthur Goldhammer, trans. (Cambridge, MA: The Belknap Press of Harvard University Press, 1989). Despite the title, this contains a fascinating section on life among the Tuscan nobles during the Italian Renaissance (called the "Eve of the Renaissance" by the French editor, since the Renaissance came later to France).

Durant, Will. *The Renaissance: A History of Civilization in Italy from 1304–1576 A.D.*, The Story of Civilization, vol. 5 (New York: Simon & Schuster, 1953). A long but lively history. While some specific facts and interpretations may be disputed by more recent historians, Durant provides specifics on many events that other histories gloss over.

Gage, John. *Life in Italy at the Time of the Medici*, European Life Series (New York: Capricorn Books, 1968). Contains fascinating chapters on life at various socioeconomic levels and on social activities such as sports and theater, as well as an excellent discussion of the role of women. The author tells much of the story through quotations from Renaissance people.

Gendel, Milton, ed. *An Illustrated History of Italy* (New York: McGraw-Hill, 1966). A heavily illustrated book with essays by noted scholars on various periods of Italian history, including "The Renaissance: Art, Humanism and Society, 1377–1559" by Peter Burke. As an added bonus, readers can get a feeling for Italy before and after the Renaissance.

Goodenough, Simon. *The Renaissance,* The Living Past (London: Marshall Cavendish, 1979). A short but informative juvenile book with two-page illustrated spreads covering various aspects of Renaissance life.

Hale, John R. *Renaissance,* Great Ages of Man (New York: Time-Life Books, 1965). The best illustrated history. Hale is a respected expert on the Italian Renaissance, who combines scholarly accuracy with a true appreciation for the glories of the time; the color illustrations are wonderful.

———, ed. *Concise Encyclopedia of the Italian Renaissance* (New York: Oxford University Press, 1981). An excellent reference book with hundreds of brief, informative entries on people, places, events, and subject areas. Many libraries will have this available for circulation.

Hearder, Harry. *Italy: A Short History* (Cambridge, England: Cambridge University Press, 1990.) A well-written, very brief history with excellent chapters on the Renaissance, as well as on the events leading up to and following the Renaissance period.

The editors of Horizon Magazine. *The Horizon Book of the Renaissance* (New York: American Heritage, 1961). The most comprehensive illustrated history; the main text by historian J. H. Plumb is delightfully readable, but not quite as up-to-date in scholarly accuracy as Hale's; also includes nine excellent biographical essays by other historians on individuals like Machiavelli, Leonardo, Michelangelo, and Isabella d'Este; the sheer number of illustrations makes this a must for any student who wants to "see" the Renaissance. There is a simpler version of this book entitled *The Golden Book of the Renaissance,* adapted for young readers by Irwin Shapiro (New York: Golden Press, 1962). Although it's worthwhile in itself, the adult version is not that difficult.

Howarth, Sarah. *Renaissance People* and *Renaissance Places* (Brookfield, CT: The Millbrook Press, 1992). Two easy-reading juvenile books that focus on types of people (The Banker, The Artist, The Alchemist) and types of places (The City, The Sculptor's Workshop, The Home). Although the text is very simple, the information is interesting.

Koch, H. W. *Medieval Warfare* (Englewood Cliffs, NJ: Prentice-Hall, 1978). Despite the title, contains excellent information and illustrations on warfare during the Renaissance, including the age of the condottieri, and on the use of artillery during the foreign invasions.

Laven, Peter. *Renaissance Italy: 1464–1534* (New York: G. P. Putnam's Sons, 1966). A scholarly book that is too difficult for young readers, but provides excellent information on subject areas such as the development of science and technology.

Lintner, Valerio. *A Traveller's History of Italy* (New York: Interlink Books, 1989). Contains good, concise historical information, an extensive chronology, and a section on historical sites in specific cities.

Martinelle, Giuseppe, ed. *The World of Renaissance Florence,* Walter Darwell, trans. (New York: G. P. Putnam's Sons, 1968). Illustrated

Italian book exploring all aspects of life in Florence during the Renaissance.

Marzieh, Gail. *Life in the Renaissance* (New York: Random House, 1968). A detailed, illustrated juvenile book with good information on daily life, including the life of young people.

BIOGRAPHIES OF INDIVIDUALS AND FAMILIES

Bernier, Oliver. *The Renaissance Princes,* Treasures of the World (Chicago: Stonehenge Press, 1983). The rather weak text focuses on the Medici, Este, and Farnese families, but the real joys of this book are the wonderful color photos of exquisite Renaissance paintings and art objects.

Brion, Marcel. *The Medici: A Great Florentine Family,* Gilles and Heather Cremonesi, trans. (New York: Crown, 1969). A comprehensive, illustrated book on the Medici family, written by a French scholar.

Burman, Edward. *Italian Dynasties: The Great Families of Italy from the Renaissance to the Present Day* (Wellingborough, Northamptonshire, England: Equation, 1989). A recent book that includes chapters on most of the important Renaissance families, with short sections on significant individuals in each family.

Erlanger, Rachel. *Lucrezia Borgia: A Biography* (New York: Hawthorn Books, 1978). Detailed biography of the woman who became a symbol of immorality for centuries to come.

————. *The Unarmed Prophet: Savonarola of Florence* (New York: McGraw- Hill, 1988). An excellent but very detailed book that sets Savonarola's reform movement in the context of Florence under Lorenzo de' Medici. The author sees Savonarola as a 15th-century version of Ayatollah Khomeini.

Haney, John. *Cesare Borgia* (New York: Chelsea House, 1987). A biography for young adult readers.

The Italian Renaissance, Exploring the Past, vol. 5 (New York: Marshall Cavendish, 1989). Short, illustrated juvenile book with good biographical information on Leonardo da Vinci, Michelangelo, and Galileo.

Johnson, Marion. *The Borgias* (New York: Holt, Rinehart and Winston, 1981). A readable account of the Borgia family by an English writer who lived in Rome.

Mee, Charles L. *Lorenzo de' Medici and the Renaissance* (New York: American Heritage, 1969). A comprehensive, illustrated juvenile book that focuses on the sociopolitical forces surrounding the life of Lorenzo the Magnificent.

Rabb, Theodore K. *Renaissance Lives: Portraits of an Age* (New York: Pantheon, 1992). Profiles of 15 unusual individuals drawn from various European countries during the Renaissance, including Titian and Catherine de' Medici from Italy. Rabb was the advisor to the PBS series *Renaissance.*

Ritchie-Calder, Peter. *Leonardo & the Age of the Eye* (New York: Simon & Schuster, 1970). Examines Leonardo's life and work—particularly his scientific and technical investigations—within the context of his time; includes over 100 drawings by Leonardo as well as illustrations drawn from books that he had access to in his own personal library.

Rowdon, Maurice. *Lorenzo the Magnificent* (Chicago: Henry Regnery, 1974). A very readable book focusing on Lorenzo but also providing interesting information on other Medicis and on Florence during their reign.

Simon, Kate. *A Renaissance Tapestry: The Gonzaga of Mantua* (New York: Harper & Row, 1988). A well-written book that interweaves the lives of the Gonzaga family with those of scholars and artists around them, including Vittorino da Feltre, Andrea Mantegna, and Leon Battista Alberti; also includes excellent section on role of women.

RENAISSANCE ART

There are many excellent individual books and series of books that include fine reproductions of Renaissance art. A recent series that should be especially appealing to young adult readers is The Library of Great Masters (Florence, Italy: Scala; and New York: Riverside Book Company, 1980s–1990s). Includes short books on individual artists, with good, brief biographical information and high-quality, glossy color reproductions of their art work.

Two other series that include some excellent volumes on Renaissance artists are the Time-Life Library of Art (New York: Time Incorporated, 1960s) and the Penguin Classics of World Art (Harmondshire, England: Penguin, 1980s; first published in Italy 1960s).

Clark, Kenneth. *The Art of Humanism* (New York: Harper & Row, 1983). Contains essays on Donatello, Paolo Uccello, Leon Battista Alberti, Andrea Mantegna, and Sandro Botticelli, with emphasis on how their artistic work reflected the philosophy of humanism.

Hartt, Frederick. *Michelangelo* (New York: Abrams, 1989). Excellent color reproductions of major paintings, as well as black and white photos of details, drawings, and sculptures.

————. *Leonardo da Vinci* (New York: Raynal; originally published Novara, Italy: Istituto Geografico De Agostini, 1956). A huge volume that contains reproductions of all Leonardo's major work.

Mariani, Valerio. *Michelangelo the Painter* (New York: Abrams, 1964). A huge volume published under the auspices of an Italian national committee honoring the 400th anniversary of Michelangelo's death; excellent color reproductions of all his paintings, including many pages of details from the Sistine Chapel ceiling.

Walsh, Meg Nottingham. "Out of the Darkness: Michelangelo's Last Judgment," *National Geographic,* vol. 185, no. 5, May 1994. A brief but excellent article with color reproductions of *The Last Judgment* after the cleaning and restoration that began in 1990; also discusses how other artists altered Michelangelo's nudes during the Counter-Reformation.

ORIGINAL RENAISSANCE NONFICTION WRITINGS

Borgia, Lucrezia and Pietro Bembo. *The Prettiest Love Letters in the World: Letters Between Lucrezia Borgia and Pietro Bembo, 1503–1519* (Boston: Godine, 1987). These letters offer fascinating insight into the elegant but overwrought style of writing in Renaissance courts and the supposedly Platonic love between men and women outside of marriage.

Castiglione, Baldassare. *The Book of the Courtier,* George Bull, trans. (Baltimore: Penguin, 1967). Along with Machiavelli's

————. *The Prince,* this was one of the most influential books written during the Italian Renaissance; quite readable and entertaining.

Clements, Robert J., ed. *Michelangelo: A Self-Portrait* (Englewood Cliffs, NJ: Prentice-Hall, 1963). A fascinating collection of Michelangelo's thoughts and opinions on just about everything, arranged by subject and drawn from some 495 letters, 343 poems and poetic fragments, and verbal statements recorded by contemporaries.

Guicciardini, Francesco. *The History of Italy,* Sidney Alexander, trans. and ed. (New York: Macmillan, 1969). An abridged English translation of the famous history of the foreign invasions completed in 1540; though too long and complex for young adults to use as a history, it's surprisingly readable, and students might read a few sections to get a feeling for how a contemporary Italian viewed the disasters in his own land.

Gundersheimer, Werner L., ed. *The Italian Renaissance* (Englewood Cliffs, NJ: Prentice-Hall, 1965). Edited selections from 11 Renaissance works, including *Oration on the Dignity of Man* by Pico della Mirandola, *The Prince* by Machiavelli, *The Courtier* by Castiglione, and *The Notebooks* of Leonardo. All the selections are very readable and provide fascinating insight into the thinking of the Renaissance.

Machiavelli, Niccolò. *The Portable Machiavelli,* Peter Bondanella and Mark Musa, eds. and trans. (New York: Viking Press, 1979). A compilation of Machiavelli's most important works in new translations; includes his private letters, *The Prince,* an abridged version of the *Discourses,* and his comic play *The Mandrake.*

————. *The Prince,* Quentin Skinner and Russell Price, eds. and trans., Cambridge Texts in the History of Political Thought (Cambridge, England, and New York: Cambridge University Press, 1988). Machiavelli's famous book is brief, quite readable, and available in many translations; other editions include translations by Harvey C. Mansfield (University of Chicago Press, 1985) and George Bull (Penguin Classics, 1961).

FICTION, RENAISSANCE AND CONTEMPORARY

Ariosto, Ludovico. *Orlando Furioso* (New York: Penguin Classics, 1975). The most popular epic poem of the later Italian Renaissance tells a tale of romance and enchantment set in the time of Charlemagne; Orlando is the Italian name for the French knight Roland, and the title literally means "Mad Roland."

Boccaccio, Giovanni. *The Decameron of Giovanni Boccaccio,* Richard Aldington, trans. (New York: Dell, 1962; originally published New York: Doubleday, 1930). Boccaccio's stories are surprisingly modern, funny, and sexy almost 650 years after they were first written.

Dante's Inferno. Mark Musa, trans. (Bloomington: Indiana University Press, 1971). An excellent, very readable translation of the first and most famous part of Dante's great epic poem, with very helpful notes.

Five Italian Renaissance Comedies, Bruce Penman, ed. (New York: Penguin Classics, 1978). A selection of 16th-century comic plays in mostly new translations; includes *The Mandragola* (*The Mandrake*) by Machiavelli, *Lena* by Ariosto, *The Stablemaster* by Aretino, *The Deceived* by Gl'Intronati, and *The Faithful Shepherd* by Guarini.

Holland, Cecelia. *City of God: A Novel of the Borgias* (New York: Knopf, 1977); Briggs, Jean, *The Flame of the Borgias* (New York: Harper & Row, 1974); and Davis, Genevieve, *A Passion in the Blood* (New York: Simon & Schuster, 1977). Three novels based on the Borgia family; see also the novels by Maugham, Plaidy, and Seymour listed below. Novelists love the intrigue and dark doings of the Borgias, but recent scholarship considers Lucrezia fairly innocent (her father and brother are a different matter).

Italian Stories, Robert A. Hall, Jr., ed. (Reprint Dover, 1989; originally published New York: Bantam, 1961). Eleven Italian short stories with the original Italian on the left-hand pages and new English translations on the right-hand pages; includes three stories by Renaissance writers: Giovanni Boccaccio, Niccolò Machiavelli, and Matteo Bandello.

Lennox, Judith. *The Italian Garden* (New York: St. Martin's Press, 1993). A recent novel set in the Renaissance period.

Maugham, W. Somerset. *Then and Now* (Garden City, NY: Doubleday, 1946). A novel about the age of Cesare Borgia and Niccolò Machiavelli by one of the finest English writers of the 20th century.

Plaidy, Jean. *Madonna of the Seven Hills* (New York: Putnam, 1974); and Seymour, Miranda, *Daughter of Shadows* (New York: Coward, McCann, & Geoghegan, 1977). Two novels based on the life of Lucrezia Borgia.

Ripley, Alexandra. *The Time Returns* (Garden City, NY: Doubleday, 1985). A novel about Lorenzo de' Medici and Florence.

Shulman, Sandra. *The Florentine,* originally published as *Francesca— the Florentine* (New York: Morrow, 1973). A novel set in Florence during the time of Lorenzo de' Medici.

FILM AND VIDEO

Grubin, David, prod. and dir. *Florence,* Power of the Past (Alexandria, VA: PBS Video, 1991). A 90-minute video in which narrator Bill Moyers examines the living power of Renaissance Florence through informal conversations with people in the streets, museums, and churches of the city; available in many libraries.

Rossellini, Roberto, dir. *The Age of Cosimo de' Medici* (Balzac Video, 1989). A two-hour video about Florence and Italy during Cosimo's time.

West, Clifford B., and Nancy Fisher, dirs. *The Medici and Palazzo Vecchio: The Florentine Republic and Ducal Florence,* Treccani Video Library, Art and Architecture Series (New York: Enao/Treccani, 1989). A half-hour video about Florence during the reign of the later Medici in the 16th century.

Zeffirelli, Franco, dir. *Romeo and Juliet* (British-Italian production, 1968). This lavish film of Shakespeare's classic play captures the colorful style of the Italian Renaissance, as well as many details of Renaissance life; the original story occurred during the late medieval conflict between Guelphs and Ghibellines in Verona, but both the play and the movie are more reflective of the 15th-century Renaissance; should be available on video in many stores and libraries.

INDEX

Boldface page numbers indicate special features. *Italic* page numbers indicate illustrations or captions.

Medici, Lorenzo de' *See* Lorenzo the Magnificent
Medici, Piero de' (father of Lorenzo) 28–29, 83, 109
Medici, Piero de' (son of Lorenzo) 32
Medici Bank 26, 27, 30, 130
Medici family 26–28, 44 *See also individual members*
medicine 1, 91, **96–99**
Mediterranean Sea 47
melody 108
metal technology 100
Michelangelo **85–87**
    aristocratic origins of 8
    David sculpted by 87, 88, 132
    Flemish painting derided by 124
    genius of 1, 30, 91
    Ghiberti's doors praised by 25, 79
    Julius II as patron of 81
    Last Judgment painted by 87, 120, 132
    longevity of 102, 133
    Paul II as patron of 121
    Sistine Chapel ceiling painted by 43, 81, 132
Milan **50–53**
    Charles VIII alliance (1494) 114–115
    emergence of 6
    Ferrara alliance 63
    Florence allied with (1454) 28
    Florence as enemy of 22, 24
    Francis I invasion of (1515) 117–118
    French conquest of (1499) 117
    French defeat in conflict over (1525) 118
    as great power 18
    in League of Cambrai (1509) 63
    in League of Venice (1495) 116
    Mantua as buffer between Venice and 60
    population growth 7
Milton, John 127
mirrors 94
mistresses 104
Mona Lisa (Leonardo da Vinci) 85, 132
money *See* currency
Montefeltro, Federigo da 63–64, 71, 75, 103
More, Sir Thomas 125, *126*
Moro, Lodovico il *See* Sforza, Lodovico "il Moro"
motion 84
music 39, 63–64, **106–108**, 123–124, 127

Naples **53–55**
    claimed by Aragon royal family 35
    claimed by Charles VIII 32, 55, 114
    Florentine invasions by 24, 30
    as great power 18
    and papal politics 40–41
    Spanish-French invasions of (1500–1509) 117
Naples, University of 54, 55
Napoleon I (France) 49
navigation 95
Neo-Platonists 96
nepotism 38
Netherlands 124–125
new learning 9
new Romans 22
New World 30, 57, 97, 114, 118
Niccoli, Niccolò 36, 74–75

Nicholas V (pope) 36, 43, 71, 73, 131
Nicolas of Cusa 96
Norwich, John Julius 14
notaries 9
Notebooks (Leonardo da Vinci) 129

Oddi family 64
Of Divine Proportion (Fra Luca Pacioli) 95
oil-based painting 84
oligarchy, Florentine 22
On the Fabric of the Human Body (Andreas Vesalius) 99
Oration on the Dignity of Man (Giovanni Pico della Mirandola) 74, 131

Pacioli, Fra Luca 95
Padua 9, 47, 57, 59, 130
Padua, University of 48, 59, 97, 99, 123
painting *See* art
Palazzo Medici (Florence) 27
Palermo (Sicily) 6, 7
Palestrina, Giovanni Pierluigi da 108
Palmieri, Matteo viii
Panzano, Luca da 104
papacy *See also* Papal States; *individual popes*
    antipopes 35
    and the arts 121
    Avignon court 11–12, 33
    Great Schism (1378–1417) 18, 34, 130, 131
    Guelph-Ghibelline rivalry 6
    Holy Roman Empire rivalry 5, 6
    League of Cambrai (1509) 48–49, 63
    Naples alliance 35
    Pazzi conspiracy 38
    Pico debate 73–74
    political popes 38–45
    Savonarola opposition 32
Papal States
    Ferrara as buffer between Venice and 60
    Florentine war with (1375–78) 34
    mid-14th-century turmoil in 33
    papal claims to 5
    rebellious cities of 43
    Robert of Anjou partial control of 54
    Urbino as independent entity within 63
    Venice alliance formed 117
    Visconti conquests in 22
parachutes 94
Paradise Lost (John Milton) 127
Paul II (pope) 37–38
Paul III (pope) 121, 132
Paul IV (pope) 121
Pavia, Battle of (1525) 118
Pavia, University of 50
Pazzi conspiracy 29–30, 38, 131
Pazzi family 29–30
Peace of Lodi (1454) *See* Lodi, Peace of (1454)
perspective (art) 25, 78–79, 83, 95, 123
Perugia 64
Petrarch, Francesco 13–17, 21, 54, 67, 68, 75, 109, 122, 130
Petrucci, Pandolfo 59
Philip II (Spain) 111, 119, 128